TRUSTING TOGETHER IN GOD

TRUSTING TOGETHER IN GOD

Living Your Faith, My Faith, and Our Faith

JAN AND MYRON CHARTIER

ABBEY PRESS
St. Meinrad, Indiana 47577

*to
David and Vera Mace
whose relationship
has nurtured and inspired us
in our marriage and faith.*

Photo Credits: H. Armstrong Roberts, Cover, page 84; Camerique, page 20; Lee Snider, page 32; Paul Buddle, page 45; Roger Neal, page 56; Florence Sharp, page 68; Dave Swan, page 122; David McConnell, page 135; Bob Taylor, page 148; Jim Whitmer, page 169.

Library of Congress Catalog Card Number
83-73132

IBSN: 0-87029-193-9

**©1984 St. Meinrad Archabbey
St. Meinrad, Indiana 47577**

CONTENTS

Introduction

1 Faith: Yours, Mine, Ours 9

2 The Many Sides of Faith 21

3 Nurturing Faith Through Self-Esteem Enrichment 33

4 Nurturing Faith Through Talking and Listening 47

5 Nurturing Faith Through Centricity 57

6 Nurturing Faith Through Caring 71

7 Nurturing Faith Through Mutual Trust 85

8 Nurturing Faith Through Mutual Need Fulfillment 97

9 Nurturing Faith Through Life's Changes 111

10 Nurturing Faith Through Crises 123

11 Nurturing Faith Through Parenting 137

12 Nurturing Faith Through Shared Experiences 149

13 Nurturing Faith Through Mutual Service 159

Afterword

Introduction

Faith issues pervade our lives. Whether we recognize them or find them comfortable, they are there! All persons have to make decisions (many times done unconsciously or with little thought) about where to place their ultimate trust in life. When we decide to whom or to what we will entrust our well-being, we are making faith decisions. The process of life entrustment is bound up with what it means to have faith.

Faith issues are involved in the relationship of every Christian couple. Sometimes these issues are ignored. However, their presence is no less real. Faith issues need to be faced and addressed. The manner in which couples deal with matters of faith is directly related to the quality of shared faith that marital partners experience in their relationship.

This book is designed to assist couples in discovering the boundaries of faith as it relates to each person in a marriage. It also aids them in discerning the shape and boundary of the faith they share together.

The book focuses on several themes. Each includes:

- some information, concepts, and ideas,
- a structured exercise for couples to do, and
- some thoughts to guide reflection and meditation.

Through the various chapters, couples will be challenged to examine their faith, think about it, and discuss it. We, as authors, hope that through the process, couples will discover deeper dimensions for vital faith living.

CHAPTER 1

FAITH: YOURS, MINE, OURS

REFLECTION

"My faith belongs to me. Your faith belongs to you. Our faith belongs to us."

What does it all mean? As a man and a woman begin the process of dating and courtship which leads to marriage, they each bring with them a faith that has been shaped and forged within the give-and-take of life experiences in their families of origin, their church communities, and their peer groups. Each has developed a unique way of viewing life and its deepest values. In the early stages of relationship building, couples often assume that their perspectives are the same. They may view any differences between them as being insignificant or irrelevant, therefore overlooking them. Over time, however, the faith perspective of one is likely to contrast so sharply with that of the other that the difference can no longer be ignored. My faith seems to stand over and against my partner's. What does it mean when my faith isn't the same as the faith of the one I love? How do we deal with this? What should we do?

The way in which mates come to grips with the likenesses and differences in the faith perceptions they each bring to the relationship will have much to do with the quality of faith they will shape and share together. In large measure, it will control to what extent faith issues remain strictly personal rather than being shared. The answer as to what is "yours, mine, and ours" in faith dynamics will vary from couple to couple. Each couple has to work out their own "best way."

The process of defining the boundaries of my faith, your faith, and our faith usually results in several kinds of answers which we call *patterns*. While it is true that each couple has to find their own pattern, it's also true that some patterns are healthier than others. Healthy patterns lead to a vital faith which not only respects both individuals, but maximizes their faith potential as a couple.

In order to explore some of the more common patterns used by couples to decide what is your faith, my faith, and our faith, imagine you are a recently married couple. You are engaged in a conversation regarding what church you will attend. As you read the dialogues, think about how the decision is being made. Who is making the decision? What feelings is each person experiencing? While the issue of which church to attend may seem simple, it's important to realize that how a couple makes this decision will reveal a great deal about how they are likely to approach deeper, more crucial issues of faith.

Some years ago we created a fictitious couple whom we call Harry and Alice. They will demonstrate the various styles through their conversations. You might gain more insight if you actually read the lines aloud, trying to capture the feelings of these two people.

A Fused Faith Relationship

Harry: "Alice, tomorrow is Sunday. Where shall we attend worship if we go?"
Alice: "Well—what do *you* think?"
Harry: "Well, I don't know. I've wondered about what we'd do. We could do several things, you know."
Alice: "It's hard to know what's best, but I suppose we might try something new."
Harry: "We might do that. It seems okay to me."
Alice: "Okay. Sounds good to me."
Harry: "Are we agreed?"
Alice: "I guess so. We're together on it."
Harry: "We sure are."
Alice: "Supper is on the table. Let's eat."
Harry: "What are we having?'
Alice: "Stew."

This couple is more concerned with deciding what to do about worship attendance, rather than dealing with their differences. They feel good about being together in their choice, but they have done little to explore the meaning of the decision. They simply move on to another topic. If they persist in dealing with faith issues in this manner, they'll likely develop a *fused faith relationship.* The emphasis is on sameness. The crucial issue isn't what faith is to be, but rather that they're alike. Any faith differences threaten this kind of relationship. It's important that "we think and feel alike." Commonality is a priority. On occasions when differences are obviously present, this couple may go to extraordinary lengths to avoid confronting the issues.

The fused faith relationship involves an intertwined kind of sharing. This couple cherishes the illusion that they hold all things in common and have no differences. They value oneness. Figure 1 illustrates their kind of faith relationship.

In a fused faith relationship, the partners do share faith, but the sharing is at the cost of unique personal faith. To such couples, separateness—in the sense of "my faith, your faith"—is dangerous. A sticky, pervasive "we-ness" permeates the "our faith" relationship. Such a couple seems to say, "We always feel and think alike when it comes to faith." They don't seem to realize that they have lost the critical dimension of personal faith.

Figure 1 ***A Fused Faith Relationship***

A Fight Faith Relationship

Harry: "Alice, tomorrow is Sunday. I think we ought to attend worship at my church."
Alice: "Hey, you just wait one minute. You've got to be crazy to think I'm going to attend your church. We will attend my church, Harry!"
Harry: "No way, Alice. You may think I'm crazy to think we ought to go to my church, but I'd be an absolute looney if I were to set foot in your church."
Alice: "And what's wrong with my church?"
Harry: "Plenty!! We will attend my church tomorrow!!"
Alice: "Harry, you are so closeminded. You've never given my church a chance. You just assume your church is best and everything else is inferior."
Harry: "Hey, you just hold on, Alice. You never change your mind. Your brother told me you are as stubborn as a mule. I believe it!"
Alice: "Why don't you shut up!"

In the *fight faith relationship,* there is constant and open battle. Couples with this relationship pattern have been unable to achieve a stable, shared faith. Each individual seeks a dominant position, and neither person is willing to submit to the other. It is an intensely competitive relationship, with a theme of "my form of spirituality is better than yours." Each seems threatened by the unique personal faith of the mate. Rather than trying to understand its dynamics, each spouse seems willing to do anything to put the other down and gain the upper hand, however temporary the apparent victory. Each spouse is reluctant to share faith stories for fear the information will be used for personal attack in the chronic battle with their spouse.

Figure 2 illustrates the kind of faith relationship that exists between such spouses.

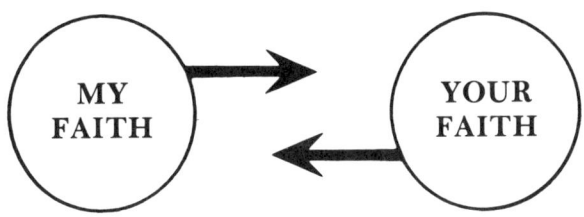

Figure 2 **A Fight Faith Relationship**

Each partner has a personal faith which must be defended against the invasion of the spouse's orientation. For such couples, faith becomes an occasion for warfare rather than a dynamic that nurtures wholeness in the marriage.

A Dominant-Submissive Faith Relationship

Harry: "Alice, tomorrow is Sunday. I've decided that we will attend worship at my church."

Alice: "But Harry, what about *my* church? When we got married, I had hoped we would at least *try* my church."

Harry: "Alice, I'm the head of this household. That responsibility belongs to me. I'm the one who's supposed to decide what's best for us spiritually."

Alice: "Before we settle on *your* church, I really think we ought to consider the virtues of *my* church. There *are* some, you know."

Harry: "Alice, where we attend worship is my decision to make. According to our marriage vows, you are to obey me. My mind is made up."

Alice: "Harry, let's not decide so quickly. Maybe we could spend some more time . . ."

Harry: "Alice, you are being totally overbearing and out of line on this issue. I'm the spiritual leader in this marriage, and you ought to respect my God-given authority. We will attend *my* church. That is my decision. Now that we've settled that, what's for dinner?"

Alice: "Your favorite dish—roast beef."

This couple reached a quick decision, but it reflected the faith orientation of the dominant husband. The *dominant-submissive pattern* of a faith relationship is found whenever one partner's views prevail, regardless of whatever validity may be present in the other's perspective. All expertise is assumed to be within the one mate, and his or her thoughts and feelings dictate the nature of "shared faith" in the relationship. This is the classical hierarchical type of relationship as illustrated in Figure 3.

Figure 3 ***A Dominant-Submissive Faith Relationship***

Some couples find this pattern completely acceptable. Many believe it has biblical authority. When both affirm it, there may be little, if any, open conflict over faith issues. Indeed, the relationship can be a highly complementary one. Both persons find their faith needs met by the relationship.

But it's not unusual that some underlying faith differences will surface from time to time. Never feeling competent and confident in matters of faith, and always giving in to the other may diminish self-worth, while anger directed at the dominant mate begins to mount. In such relationships, deeper matters of faith aren't shared with one's spouse. The dominant mate is reluctant to share doubts, fears, or uncertainties about a variety of faith issues for fear that such sharing will be perceived as weakness and "used against me." The submissive spouse, already feeling inadequate, fears being put down even further by the disclosure of "my struggles with faith realities." Neither has the capacity to share faith at a deep, intimate level. Shared faith will take place at less risky levels—for example, in pedantic discussions of doctrine or in decisions about participation in church activities. The struggles of the soul are likely to be locked tightly inside. After all, sharing one's private world of faith makes one vulnerable and could be dangerous.

A Distributed Faith Relationship

Harry: "Alice, tomorrow is Sunday. We need to talk about where we will attend worship—at my church or your church."

Alice: "Oh, that's a problem, given how we are so committed to our own churches."

Harry: "Well, Honey, what do you want to do?"

Alice: "Harry, I would really like to attend services at my church. All my friends are there. The pastor has ministered to me through some very important crises. If I go, will you go with me?"

Harry: "Alice, that's impossible; you know that. I'm scheduled to read the Old Testament reading in the service at my church."

Alice: "Well, I guess that means you'll go to your church, and I'll go to my church. Do you feel okay about that?"

Harry: "Yes and No! I really would like it if we shared a common church, but given the strength of our commitments to each of our churches, it feels fine. I respect you and your church, and I know you respect me and my church. That mutual respect for our faith traditions is important to me."

Alice: "I agree. Supper is on; let's eat."

This couple were able to tell each other about their faith commitment as it related to worship attendance on a given Sunday. They agreed that each would "do their own thing." If this pattern persists with respect to other religious questions, the couple will develop what is called a *distributed faith relationship.* They're able to confront and respect their differences, but given the intensity of their faith commitments and traditions, they're virtually unable to experience shared faith. What they do share is respect for the integrity of each other's beliefs, attitudes, and conduct. In a sense, they agree to disagree. This faith relationship is diagrammed in Figure 4.

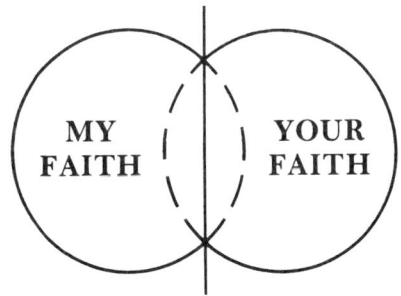

Figure 4 ***A Distributed Faith Relationship***

The overlapping area with the dotted lines represents the couple's decision to disagree, but to respect one another. The solid vertical line shows that each person's faith is indeed unique and personal in nature. However, it isn't an experience shared with one's spouse. A distributed faith relationship allows persons to pursue their own faith conviction and development with the full respect of their partner.

This pattern holds much in common with the shared faith relational pattern. The similarities and differences will be clarified by the following dialogue and discussion.

A Shared Faith Relationship

Harry: "Alice, tomorrow is Sunday. We need to talk about where we'll attend worship — at my church or your church."

Alice: "Harry, that may be a problem given our strong feelings for our own churches."

Harry: "Well, Honey, I understand that, but more than anything else I want us to be able to share a common faith commitment."

Alice: "Harry, are you saying that it's your church or else?"

Harry: "Oh, no, not at all, Alice. I just want worship attendance to be a shared part of our marriage. If that means I go to your church, okay. But maybe we could find a new church that can become *our* church."

Alice: "I share your desire that worship be at the core of our marriage, but I will find it difficult to give up my church."

Harry: "So will I, but I wouldn't want to force you to attend my church even if I could. And I really don't want you coercing me."

Alice: "Maybe we should try each other's church for a period of time, and then try some others before we make a mutual decision about where we will nurture our faith in God."

Harry: "I like that. Let's go to your church tomorrow."

Alice: "Suits me. Let's eat; I'm starved."

In a *shared faith relationship,* both husband and wife respect the faith integrity of the other. They see each other as unique, but competent in matters of faith commitment. In their desire to create a mutually shared faith, they openly share their faith convictions and feelings. They have no need to dominate each other, to put the other down, or to consume each other. They do have a need to be spiritually intimate. They don't want their faith experience to be a lonely one. They want to share it with their life partner. The diagram in Figure 5 illustrates the dynamic of this faith relationship.

Figure 5 **A Shared Faith Relationship**

For the area of shared faith to develop, a couple will need to talk and listen to each other carefully. Through face-to-face communication, their common faith will be discovered. From there, they'll have to make some decisions about how faith will be shared. But even as their shared faith grows and expands, personal faith will be respected and encouraged.

* * * * *

The dialogues you have just read have been brief. They have all centered on what church to attend. Many other faith issues could have been chosen. The purpose of the dialogues is to help you see patterns of relating that are fundamentally different. These relational patterns are used to decide many life issues besides those relating to faith. We trust you were able to see the health and "unhealth" for Harry and Alice in the various patterns.

In this book, we will advocate a shared faith that includes:

- My Faith
- Your Faith
- Our Faith

It's our belief that a shared faith relationship will produce a high quality of spiritual intimacy which will nurture both personal faith and shared faith.

EXERCISE

Instructions: Following are two sets of the same exercise—one for each marital partner. Each complete one without discussion. For example, you might write, "I am devout, a person of action, etc. You are pious, caring, etc. We are churchgoers, prayerful, etc." After each of you has completed as much as you can, read what the other has written and discuss your similarities and differences. Then take some time to consider these discussion questions.

1. What do you affirm about yourselves as persons of faith?

2. To what degree is the life of faith a shared experience in your marriage? How comfortable are you with what you see? Why?

3. What ways of being faith persons and partners would you like to change or improve?

Wife

My Faith: As a person of faith, I am:

1. _____
2. _____
3. _____
4. _____
5. _____

Your Faith: As a person of faith, you are:

1. _____
2. _____
3. _____
4. _____
5. _____

Our Faith: As persons of faith, we are:

1. _____
2. _____
3. _____
4. _____
5. _____

Husband

My Faith: As a person of faith, I am:

1. _____
2. _____
3. _____
4. _____
5. _____

Your Faith: As a person of faith, you are:

1. _____
2. _____
3. _____
4. _____
5. _____

Our Faith: As persons of faith, we are:

1. _____
2. _____
3. _____
4. _____
5. _____

MEDITATION

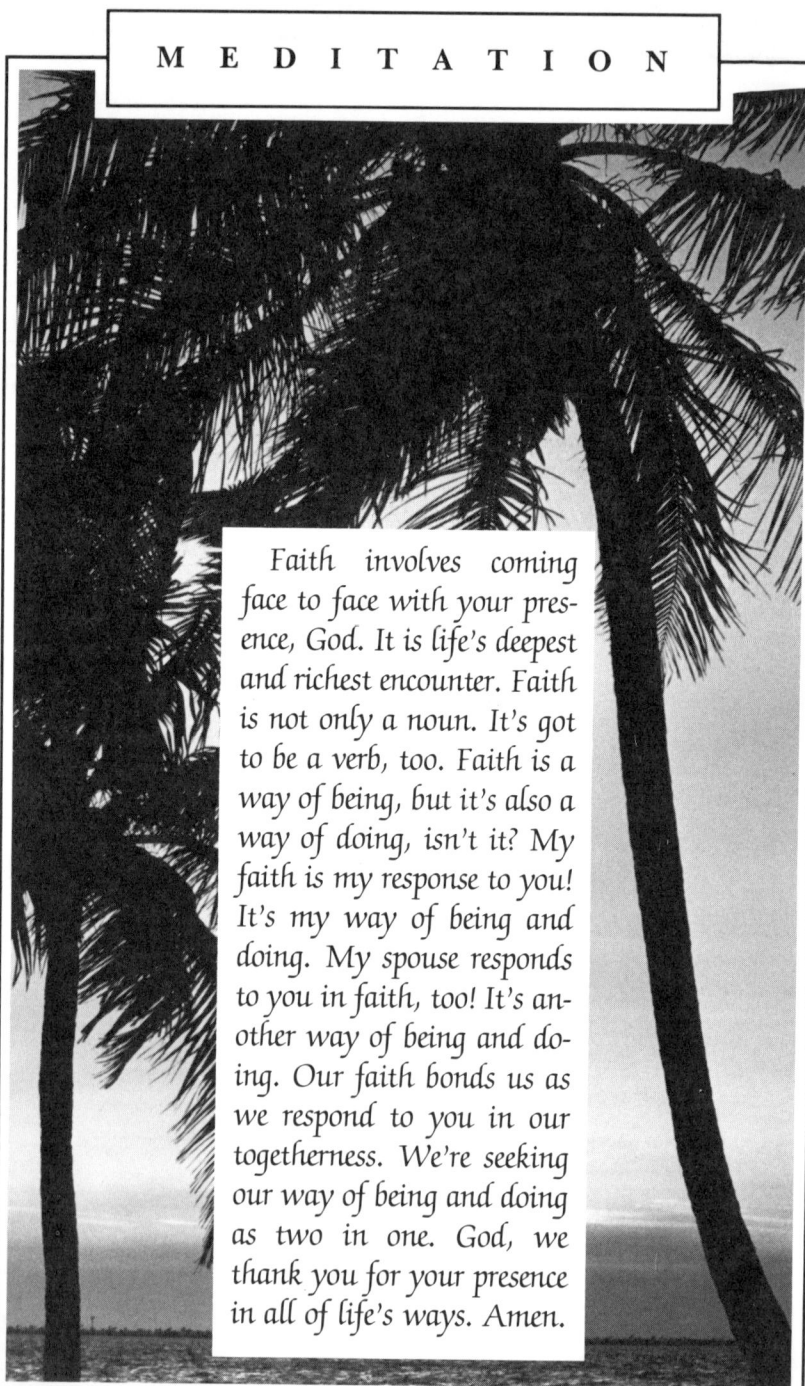

Faith involves coming face to face with your presence, God. It is life's deepest and richest encounter. Faith is not only a noun. It's got to be a verb, too. Faith is a way of being, but it's also a way of doing, isn't it? My faith is my response to you! It's my way of being and doing. My spouse responds to you in faith, too! It's another way of being and doing. Our faith bonds us as we respond to you in our togetherness. We're seeking our way of being and doing as two in one. God, we thank you for your presence in all of life's ways. Amen.

CHAPTER 2

THE MANY SIDES OF FAITH

REFLECTION

What is the nature of our faith? What is faith all about? In many services of worship, Christians proclaim their faith by saying:

"I believe in God, the Father Almighty, creator of heaven and earth. I believe in Jesus Christ, his only Son, our Lord. He was conceived by the power of the Holy Spirit and born of the Virgin Mary. He suffered under Pontius Pilate, was crucified, died, and was buried. He descended to the dead. On the third day he rose again. He ascended into heaven, and is seated at the right hand of the Father. He will come again to judge the living and the dead. I believe in the Holy Spirit, the holy catholic Church, the communion of saints, the forgiveness of sins, the resurrection of the body, and the life everlasting. Amen.*

Faith as a Belief System

The Apostles' Creed is a statement of profound and central belief affirmations. Faith is and can be a system of religious beliefs. How is such faith nurtured? Given such a definition, the object of faith enrichment would be to help people develop strong convictions. A book about nurturing a strong system of beliefs could be very legitimate, but it might not be too interesting to many Christian couples.

Christian faith is more than a belief system. It isn't contained within a set of ideas or doctrines. Growth in the faith is much deeper and greater than believing the right concepts about God, humanity, and the world. A person can verbally confess all the great creeds of the church and still miss the essence of Christian faith.

Faith as Religious Feelings

In recent years, much emphasis has been placed on religious experience as the basis of faith. There is no question that faith has an experiential and emotional dimension. However, a person can have profound emotional experiences which may seem to be religious in nature, but which fail to reconcile one with God, neighbor, self, and the world. Faith enrichment from this perspective might degenerate into creating bogus religious experiences that give people an emotion-

---

*English translation of the *Apostles' Creed* by the International Consultation on English Text.

al high. There is no question that genuine Christian faith is capable of generating deep emotional experiences within people. But like correct beliefs, emotional highs alone don't contain the essence of Christian faith. God doesn't steer the universe or me personally by emotional impulses.

Faith as Moral Behavior

During the 1960s, faith was seen as high ideals expressed in moral conduct. Values and morality expressed in righteous behavior have always had their place in Hebrew and Christian faith. "Faith without works is dead" has a long tradition. Christian faith has within it a strong moral and ethical dimension, but right conduct alone doesn't capture the basic essence of our faith.

Even if we were to add right belief, strong emotional experience, and moral conduct together, the sum would still fail to come to the essence of Christian faith.

If these three elements by themselves or added together

$$\text{RIGHT BELIEF + EMOTIONAL EXPERIENCE + MORAL CONDUCT} \neq \text{CHRISTIAN FAITH}$$

don't make for Christian faith, what does? What is the essence of faith?

To obtain an understanding of the fundamental nature of faith, we need to understand it from a biblical perspective—both Old and New Testaments.

Faith as a Trusting Relationship

One of the difficulties in understanding the nature of faith is rooted in the English language which uses the word "faith" as a noun. However, from the perspective of the Bible, faith is primarily a verb. It means to rely upon God, to trust God, to believe in God, and to have confidence in God. In the Old Testament "to have faith" is to entrust oneself to Yahweh and Yahweh's promises.

Abraham—a Model of Faith

Abraham is a model of faith as trust. At a time when he and his wife Sarah were childless, God appeared to him in a vision and promised to give them a son from whom would spring in time a great people (GN 15:1-5). "Abram put his trust in the LORD; and because of this the LORD was pleased with him and accepted him."

Trusting God means believing that God's promises are true. But, they can only be true if God is faithful in the promises made.

This story of promise needs to be understood in relationship to Genesis 22, the story of the sacrificial offering of Isaac. Although the explicit vocabulary of believing/trusting isn't used in this account, the incident is all about faith. God commands Abraham to sacrifice the child of promise, even though Isaac had been given as an extraordinary gift when Abraham and Sarah were too old to expect a child. By offering Isaac as a sacrifice, Abraham surrenders the gift, returning him to God. When he has demonstrated that he can make this sacrifice and yields any claim upon the child being his own possession, Isaac is permitted to live, to carry on the line of Abraham, and indeed to inherit the promise.

Abraham's son is his whole life—his name, his fortune, his future, the most precious thing he has—the one possession he really would not want and could not afford to forsake. His own life could easily be given up instead of the boy's. However, his own life wouldn't be enough. The heart and center of Abraham's world must be surrendered to God. God must become the center, and Abraham must live in absolute dependence upon God and in absolute commitment to God's will.

From the experience of Abraham and Sarah, we learn that faith is grateful acceptance of gifts freely given by God, and willing surrender of them to God's will. Faith is the absolute entrustment of one's life to the care of God.

For the Hebrew people, the issue was not whether to believe in the existence of God (that was taken for granted). The issue was whether to rely upon God as Savior and Lord, to believe God's chosen mediators and the promises communicated, and to trust God as constantly willing and capable of fulfilling those promises. Such faith was the foundation of commitment to God and God's demands. Indeed, faith was incomplete if it failed to produce such commitment.

The people of Israel were expected by the spokespersons for God to rely completely on their God and the promises they had been given. If they failed to show this kind of trust, their very existence would be threatened. For Israel, God alone deserved to be trusted. Only God was completely trustworthy.

From the perspective of the Old Testament, faith is primarily an interpersonal relationship between God and person. The nature of this relationship is one of entrustment. Human beings trust God because God is absolutely trustworthy.

Christ—The Object of Faith

In the New Testament, the idea of faith being a trust relationship continues. What then emerges is the centricity of Jesus Christ as the object of faith. Faith is trust in Jesus and God's power actively at work through him as the Christ. We trust Jesus because God has come to us in his birth, life, death, resurrection, and exaltation. Jesus Christ is God's grace-gift to us. This gift evokes a response of faith within us, for Jesus awakens trust. He summons individuals to saving faith in God through their concrete interpersonal encounters with himself. Such saving faith provides confidence against fear and doubt.

Faith in the New Testament is a decision to enter into a trusting relationship with God as revealed in the redemptive activity of Jesus Christ. Indeed, in this relationship we are seized by God's love to be God's people. This trust relationship involves much more than mere intellectual assent to creeds and doctrines. This faith relationship involves a total response of belief, trust, and obedience in and to Jesus Christ, the Son of God. It calls for a response of loving him with our whole being.

Trusting Faith as It Relates to Belief, Feelings, and Conduct

Although faith is essentially relational in nature, it does involve a system of beliefs, deep emotional feelings, and moral conduct. The structure of belief systems grows out of our relational experiences with the living Christ. Christian doctrine is always rooted in the reality of God's encounters with God's people, for faith is much more than intellectual abstractions. Doctrinal systems need always to point to the reality of the experience of God's people with the Holy One. Yet beliefs do not provide us a literal, one-to-one account of the formal "object" of faith—God.

Since being related to Jesus Christ is interpersonal in nature, feelings are going to be involved like they are in any relationship of depth and consequence. In our walk with God through Christ, there will be moments when God's presence will be intense, and we will feel like we are being consumed by fire. There will be occasions when God will seem far away. The Voice will be silent. Absolute trust in the midst of a dark void is all that will keep us going.

Warm intimacy will be ours to experience. Rage and anger will also be ours when we don't understand the Lord's will in the midst of terrible situations. We'll know joy as well as sadness, exhilaration as well as despair, and confidence as well as uncertainty. Since faith rests upon a trust relationship with God in Jesus Christ, our feelings can be high or low. Our future security rests not upon the mercurial nature of our emotions, but upon the solid rock of a trusting relationship.

The life of trust in God is always expressed in moral conduct. Believing and trusting in God and faithfulness to God's ways are intimately related. To trust God requires action. Indeed, it involves a radical reorientation of one's entire way of life. Trust in God works itself out in the form of love and justice for others.

God's nature is faithfulness, which makes it possible for us to trust in response. This faithful, genuine God requires trustworthiness in humanity's deeds and actions. Faith and life are intricately interconnected.

This faith relationship with God is an interpersonal relationship with Jesus Christ that is expressed through beliefs, emotions, and conduct.

A faith relationship in Jesus Christ involves a whole-life response. It affects the whole of a person's existence. Faith is an active mode of relating to and committing oneself to Jesus Christ. Faith in Jesus is a way of moving into and giving shape to one's total life experience. Faith is being in a trustworthy relationship with Jesus Christ; it's to entrust one's life destiny to him.

Faith as Personal

Such a faith relationship with the Lord of life is intensely personal. A trusting relationship with God encompasses the totality of human life. By trusting completely, I allow God to touch all the dimensions of my being. If God is to impact all of me, then I must know myself—who I am and what I am about. How can I relate God's presence to all the dimensions of my personal being—my humanity, sexuality, self-understanding, mortality, or guilt—unless I first see what these dimensions of myself are and know something about them? How can I appropriate the promises of God to the whole of my life unless I have a rich self-knowledge?

Self-knowledge places me upon my knees and allows me to see my need for faith in a reliable God whose promises are to be trusted. Self-knowledge is very necessary for a wholistic faith. If Jesus Christ is to be the Lord of life (all of it), then I must understand myself in order to appropriate the fullness of my relationship with him. As he becomes the center of every dimension of my life—my thoughts, my feelings, my actions—I know myself even more deeply. For in a very real sense, self-knowledge is relational. I understand myself only as I am known and possessed by God in Christ. My identity and my existence depend upon my willingness to live by trust in the promises of God.

Faith as Communal

Christian faith is also deeply communal. When God called Abram, a Babylonian shepherd prince from the city of Haran in Mesopotamia, God was creating a community of faithing people. Some centuries later, this faith relationship with the God of Abraham, Isaac, and Jacob received new impetus when Moses, in the name of this God, led Abraham's oppressed descendants in the Nile delta out of Egyptian slavery. The judges and the kings formed the tribes of Israel into a nation under the sovereignty of God. Later, God formed a new people in Jesus Christ, the church.

The church as community is responsible for nurturing faith, hope, and love. A community of faith isn't a passive group of individuals. Rather, it has a primary role to play in an ongoing process of conversion and transformation. A faithing community is a community that constantly remembers its traditions and values, and renews its convictions and its trust in one another.

In the Bible, the community of faith is understood as the family of God. God is our loving parent. Jesus Christ is our elder brother. We are brothers and sisters in Christ. The Hebrews saw the family as the starting place for the formation and development of trust in God (Dt 6:4-9). Martin Luther understood the family to be a little church. Whenever a husband, wife, and children trust God absolutely, a community of faith exists. Within that familial relationship, faith can be formed and nurtured. Trusting relationships within marriage and family provide the soil out of which reliance upon God springs forth and is cultivated.

Faith as Historical

A faith relationship with God in Jesus Christ is historical in nature, involving the past, present, and future.

Past Memory

Faith in God involves the *memory* of God's previous acts of deliverance. The idea of remembrance was basic to Hebrew faith. The faithing community was admonished to remember and not to forget God's great power in liberating the Hebrews from slavery in Egypt. This faithful people lived life in light of the Exodus.

The early church remembered the cross and the resurrection. They broke bread and drank from the cup in memory of their Lord (1 Cor 11:23-25).

Christian faith is rooted in its remembrance of the Wounded Healer. Each person who has a trusting relationship with God has redemptive memories, personal experiences of faith that remind them of the source of trust.

Present Obedience

Faith in God involves living a life of trusting *obedience* in the present. Obedient action is based upon previous remembrances of God's activity in the community of faith and one's life.

Future Promise

Faith in God also means trusting that he will fulfill his *promises*. Trusting him is an act of hope for the future. God has come in Jesus Christ to begin the process of salvation, but that process is incomplete. Salvation is still a *promise* to be fulfilled.

This applies also to each person of faith. In each person who trusts Christ for salvation, the process has begun but is incomplete. Salvation has come, is coming, and will come. Faith is the integrating factor for a people living by God's promises between the times en route to a heavenly destiny.

Faith as a Growth Process

Biblical faith isn't a static condition of life or consciousness, but rather a dynamic activity of the mind, heart, and will. Faith in God isn't a virtue or condition perfectly or permanently achieved, but a relational commitment that needs continual renewal. Rather than being a human achievement it's a trusting response to God's grace gift, Jesus Christ. Since the gospel finds its ultimate expression in the cross of the Lord, our faith must constantly measure itself by this norm.

Faith in Christ is a dynamic movement which involves adjustment, change, and growth. As a faithing people, we constantly struggle between faith and unbelief. It's a lifelong struggle as we seek to live out the life of faithfulness in relationship to a trustworthy God. As we trust the promises of God and act upon them, our faith is deepened and enriched. Thus, trust builds upon trust. As we discern and do the will of God, that will becomes ever more apparent and our faith relationship with God in Christ moves to deeper and deeper levels.

Faith is a developmental process. Indeed, trust relationships don't grow as the result of biological maturation, or of necessity. Relationships have to be nurtured, or they stagnate. Growth in faith can be nurtured by intentional activities such as prayer, fellowship, study, and spiritual disciplines. It can also be nurtured through situations of crisis—moments when life places us at the boundaries of our existence. Of course, such situations potentially can rupture the bonds of trust. But for Christians wanting to grow, they can be the soil in which deep faith in God is rooted.

* * * * *

In this chapter, we have explored the many sides of faith. We have seen that faith is primarily a trusting relationship. We've also explored the faith relationship as being intensely personal and also deeply communal. We've noted that a faith relationship with Jesus Christ is historical, involving past memories, obedience in the present, and promise for the future. And, finally, we've observed that faith is subject to growth and development.

We will devote the remainder of this book to enriching the shared faith of the married couple, the micro-community of faith. Many of the sides of faith we have considered will be explored in greater depth and from different perspectives, as we point to ways to nurture your faith as a couple.

EXERCISE

Instructions: Below are two sets of unfinished statements to challenge you, as a couple, to reflect on your faith. Think about each item, making notes. Discuss your insights.

Husband

1. Some of my deepest faith beliefs are:

2. A time when I was keenly aware of the emotions related to my faith was:

3. Some ways in which I try to live out my faith in action are:

4. My commitments to grow in my own faith relationship to Jesus Christ and in our shared faith are:

    My own faith relationship:

    Our communal faith relationship:

Wife

1. Some of my deepest faith beliefs are:

2. A time when I was keenly aware of the emotions related to my faith was:

3. Some ways in which I try to live out my faith in action are:

4. My commitments to grow in my own faith relationship to Jesus Christ and in our shared faith are:

    My own faith relationship:

    Our communal faith relationship:

MEDITATION

Thou dost keep him in perfect peace,
whose mind is stayed on Thee,
because he trusts in Thee.

Trust in the Lord forever,
for the Lord God is
an everlasting rock.

Is 26:3-4

Prayer:
> We are trusting you,
> O God, to guide us.
> Help our unbelief.
> Amen.

CHAPTER 3

NURTURING FAITH THROUGH SELF-ESTEEM ENRICHMENT

REFLECTION

The following is a plan guaranteed to ruin your marriage:
1. Spy on your spouse. Observe your mate's behavior, especially shortcomings and weaknesses. Collect these observations so they can be used at strategic moments.
2. Shotgun blast. Attack your spouse from all sides. List and refer to all elements in his or her personality which reflect weakness. In three minutes, point up all personal faults, the bad aspects of his or her relatives, job, friends. Dramatize how much you have suffered as a result.
3. Tease. Be friendly on the surface, acting as if everything is a joke. Allude to tension points just enough to let your partner know "that you know." If your spouse becomes angry, respond by saying, "What's the matter, don't you have a sense of humor?" or "Hey, can't you take a joke? Why are you always so defensive?"
4. Blow up. Come on strong over some small weakness or shortcoming in your spouse. Then, justify your action on the basis of all your spouse's shortcomings you have overlooked in the past.
5. Use sex as a weapon. Don't overlook using subtle comparisons. Indicate that your mate is abnormal in some way—frigid, oversexed, or the like. Fake headaches, illnesses, or tiredness. Play games—flirt, tease, stimulate, then reject and decline.
6. Insist on openness and frankness at all times. Don't suppress your feelings or contain your expression of opinions and attitudes. Bring up things that annoy you. Get everything out into the open and be direct. Inflict pain while justifying your behavior by insisting upon the need for open, frank communication in your marriage.
7. Promise anything, do nothing. Whenever your mate asks for help, offer it, and then don't do it. Be sure your actions and your words don't match.
8. Tune out. When your spouse initiates conversation, don't listen. Walk away, avoid eye contact, and abruptly change the subject, or refuse to talk about it. Give your spouse the impression, "You're not worth communicating with." Rationalize your own behavior with the idea that "I'm too busy and have more important things to do."
9. Analyze your mate. Employ this technique to classify and label your partner. You may use simple terms like inadequate, insecure, defensive, or rigid. If you think something more sophisticated is needed, call your spouse neurotic, abnormal, or even sadistic.

10. Use physical abuse. Whenever you feel outmaneuvered by your spouse and it seems that you're losing an argument, resort to slapping, punching, kicking, scratching, biting, and/or hair pulling. Defend your behavior with the rationalization, "My spouse needs that every once in a while."

Interpersonal actions of this type are bound to bring about the ruination of a marriage. Indeed, each behavior is designed to cut into the worth and well-being of the other.

Self-Esteem and Trust

Divorce is a crisis of both self-identity and faith, and the two are interrelated. Marriage as well as a relationship with God is built upon trust. Both require trusting attitudes and behaviors.

The foundation for trust in human behavior is self-esteem — a collage of feelings about one's personal worth. To be more precise, self-esteem is the degree to which individuals regard themselves as praiseworthy and approve of and/or accept themselves. Trusting attitudes and behaviors require high self-esteem in persons. Individuals with low self-worth feelings tend to be mistrusting and suspicious of other people.

The Importance of Self-Esteem in Marriage and Faith

To understand the impact of self-esteem as it relates to marriage and faith, we need to comprehend the extent to which persons' self-esteem influences such matters as the friends they choose, the marriage partners they select, their productivity, the use they make of their abilities and aptitudes, their attitude toward creation and God, and their overall happiness in the midst of life's realities.

High Self-Esteem

High self-esteemers are basically self-affirming. They have a basic confidence about who they are. They are accepting of themselves, yet they remain realistic about both their strengths and limitations. They are happy with their uniqueness as individuals.

High self-esteemers tend to be productive, competent persons. Such individuals often are academically sharp, creative, and/or leadership-oriented. They aren't threatened easily by criticism or failure, and are able to cope with frustration. Far from being intimidated by difficult situations, they welcome the challenge of ambiguity, uncertainty, and complexity. Such persons enjoy solving problems.

High self-esteemers, rather than being isolated and lonely, enjoy other people and are eager to become involved with them. They take the initiative in interpersonal relations. They tend to be warm, assertive, caring, reliable, and trusting toward others. As a result, they have the capacity to form intimate, caring relationships. In short, they exercise a great degree of interpersonal competence.

These joyful, affirming persons have a positive view of life and God. They readily approach the tasks and chores of daily living with an underlying attitude of hope. This attitude empowers them to establish remote, not easily attainable, but highly rewarding goals. Such men and women trust their ability to cope with their environment and all its problems.

Persons of faith with high self-esteem have an image of God as loving, accepting, and caring. Faith for them is a matter of joy and celebration and goes beyond simple agreement with doctrinal formulations. Faith is anchored in an interpersonal relationship with Eternal Love.

Also, such persons have moral fortitude and are able to stand up for their convictions. Relatively free of the crippling feelings of self-inflicted guilt, their basic orientation is an empathic concern for others. Indeed, they frequently feel more troubled by their inability to resolve the larger social problems of inequality, suffering, and injustice — to resolve the discrepancy between what is and what ought to be — than by the burden of unresolved guilt and anxiety over their own behavior.

High Self-Esteemers and Marriage

When high self-esteemers enter marriage, they bring to the relationship a great deal of strength. High self-esteem couples have a large capacity for making their marriages a success. In a recent study on successful marriages, James R. Hine (*What Comes After You Say, "I Love You,"* 1980) discovered that "many marriages are successful because in them couples meet crises successfully, show affection, are loyal and faithful to each other, are alert to the importance of giving each other support and reinforcement, communicate truthfully and openly, share similar values and goals, and admire and respect each other" (p. 45).

In many ways, these characteristics describe high self-esteemers. For marriage to be rewarding, a positive sense of self is required. This truth can be seen more clearly when high self-esteemers are contrasted with low self-esteemers.

Low Self-Esteem

Low self-esteemers are self-putdowners; they're convinced of their inferiority and unlovableness. Placing unreasonable demands upon themselves, they are strongly critical and self-punishing when they fail. Aiming for unrealistic goals serves only to magnify their weaknesses.

Low self-esteemers perceive others as competent, talented, and able but fail to see such qualities in themselves. They lack belief in the abilities they have. As a result, they tend to be unproductive. Being preoccupied with self-doubt, such persons expect to fail in whatever they attempt and thereby adopt a why-try attitude. Indeed, much of their energy is often channeled into inventing highly creative ways to fail.

Low self-esteemers are highly anxious in social situations and lack confidence in their relationship-building abilities. Indeed, they tend to be shy, withdrawn, indifferent, aloof, undependable, and distrustful of others. Being on the sidelines of social activity, they are loners. They often project their self-hatred upon others in prejudicial ways. Such persons often want the affection of others but are unable to give the care, affirmation, and trust that are prerequisites for intimate relationships.

These isolated, unhappy people often have a negative view of life and of God. They're usually anxious about the future and bored with life. In fact, life is often quite meaningless for them. They tend to see God as rejecting, punitive, and impersonal. Their low self-worth seems to require a God who punishes, rather than one who loves even the unlovely.

Low Self-Esteemers and Marriage

When low self-esteemers marry, they usually experience some unhealthy marital dynamics. They enter marriage with high hopes and little trust. Because of their feelings of low self-worth, they hope to complete themselves by drawing upon the other's qualities. They also try to raise their own self-worth by making their spouse an extension of themselves.

If both spouses are low self-esteemers, they each operate on the assumption that they must please their spouse. Neither can communicate when displeased or unhappy with the other, or acknowledge disagreement or criticism directly. They fear self-disclosure lest they be seen as weak, inadequate, or — worst of all — undesirable! Low self-esteem couples act as if they are and must be indistinguishable from each other. Having a fused relationship, they use the same bloodstream, the same survival pipeline.

Whereas high self-esteemers find themselves most masterful and creative in sexual behaviors, low self-esteemers do not. Their need to feel worthwhile is so strong that married couples will go without sexual fulfillment or fail to seek it if they perceive sexual behavior or demands for it as threatening self-worth. For such mates, the need to protect self-esteem has a greater personal priority than sexual needs. Low self-esteem persons must view themselves as worthy and sexually desirable before they can experience the freedom and trust so critical to erotic feelings and sexual response.

Moments of sexual intimacy expose both partners physically and emotionally. It's very difficult to be open, relaxed, and spontaneous when a person fears rejection. Such fear presents the need to hide or withhold parts of oneself from the other. How can someone who feels inadequate, unattractive, unlovable, and unworthy trust his or her spouse to be loving and accepting? Such persons have tremendous difficulty asking for something, giving what's requested, or accepting what's offered. Low self-esteemers carefully protect themselves from an expected rejection by rejecting first.

Low self-esteem couples marry to receive from the other. They expect to give little. They believe they have little or nothing to give. Eventually they end up receiving little, too. Their bankrupt relationship only increases feelings of low self-esteem. As these feelings increase, each person in the relationship discovers a need to defend what little esteem they have. The final act of defense may very well be to file for divorce.

Middle Self-Esteem

Most persons are neither high self-esteemers, who have relatively few self-worth battles, nor low self-esteemers, who wallow in floods of self-doubt and despair continually. Rather, most people fall somewhere in between and can be categorized as middle self-esteemers.

Such persons struggle with self-doubt. They often have questions about their value and feel they must earn the love of others. Rather than taking venturesome risks, such persons play it safe in order to protect their feelings of self-worth. To avoid failure, they tend to be conformists and are compliant toward others—especially authority figures—because they depend on interpersonal acceptance to confirm their worthiness.

Middle self-esteemers can be expressive and take some criticism.

They have an average amount of confidence, given their relatively stable, contented self-feelings. As a result, they have moderate capacities and achievements in academics, leadership, and creativity.

Middle self-esteemers use social situations to support their sense of worth. They seek approval from others to erase self-doubt about their ultimate value. This approval is their key to personal well-being. Often middle self-esteemers are people-pleasers. Having a driving ambition to succeed, they are status seekers—never quite satisfied, and continually playing a role to please others. When others reject or criticize them, self-doubt raises its ugly head.

These uncertain persons have a more optimistic view of life and of God than do the low self-esteemers. Considering life an arena in which they must prove themselves, they engage in a continuous struggle between achievement and approval on the one hand, and failure and self-questioning on the other.

While such persons give intellectual assent to the forgiving love of God as important to their belief system, their Christian life is lived according to the law of achievement on an emotional and behavioral level. Grace is a theological concept, rather than a personal experience. Religious faith is a matter of status rather than a platform for creative, committed discipleship.

Middle Self-Esteemers and Marriage

Middle self-esteemers enter marriage with a mix of strengths and limitations. They have the capacity to give and the need to receive from their mate. They desperately need their spouse's approval. Because they find criticism hard to take, these persons give to their mate out of the need to build up their own self-worth. They have a limited capacity to cope successfully with crises, show affection, be loyal and faithful to each other, give each other support and positive reinforcement, communicate truthfully and openly, and share values and goals. The greatest danger for such married couples is a negative communication pattern. Such a pattern can create a negative thought cycle that reinforces feelings of low worth. Figure 1 illustrates this concept.

Such marital relationships become stagnant, characterized by boredom and eventually pain. Also, they offer little reward and can cause one of the marital partners, if not both, to question the value of the marriage and its future. Indeed, a spouse can quit a marriage out of a desperate need to protect self-worth from further damage and in the hope of finding ways to reaffirm the value of oneself.

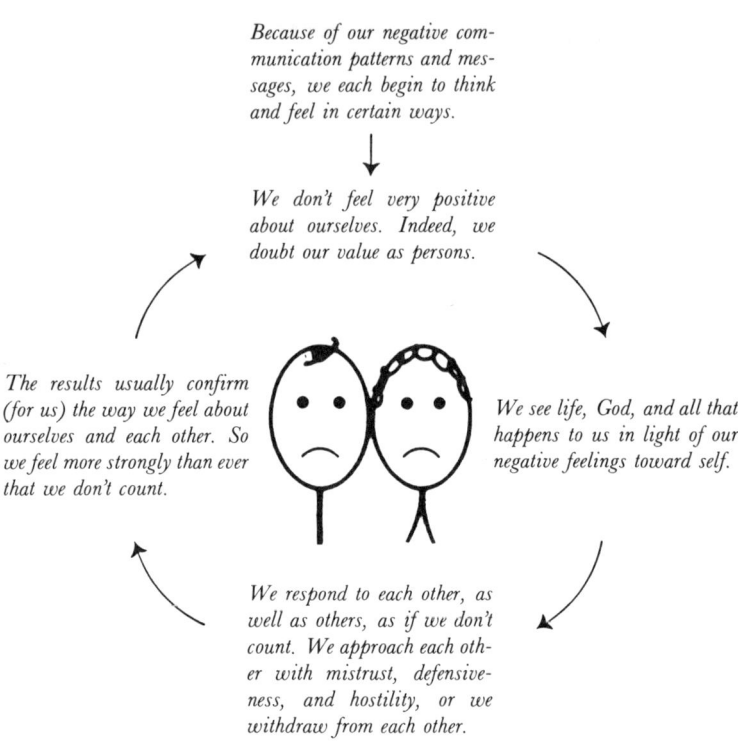

Figure 1 **The Negative Thought Cycle of Low Self-Esteem**

Guardians of Each Other's Self-Esteem

When two people marry, the marriage vows should imply the commitment to protect, as well as to affirm, the self-esteem of the other. Self-worth feelings are gained through our interaction with the primary people in our lives. As children, these primary people are parents and family. As adolescents, they are our peer group. As married persons, our spouse is the most significant "other" in our lives. Feelings of self-worth are confirmed and shaped in our marital interaction. Figure 2 illustrates this two-way interchange.

We learn our self-feelings through interaction. Our communication is shaped and molded by our self-feelings. It's a process that can be highly rewarding and exhilarating, or painful and devastating. As couples, we are like mirrors to one another. We are unable to perceive our own worth until it has been reflected back to us in the mirror of another person—our loving, caring spouse.

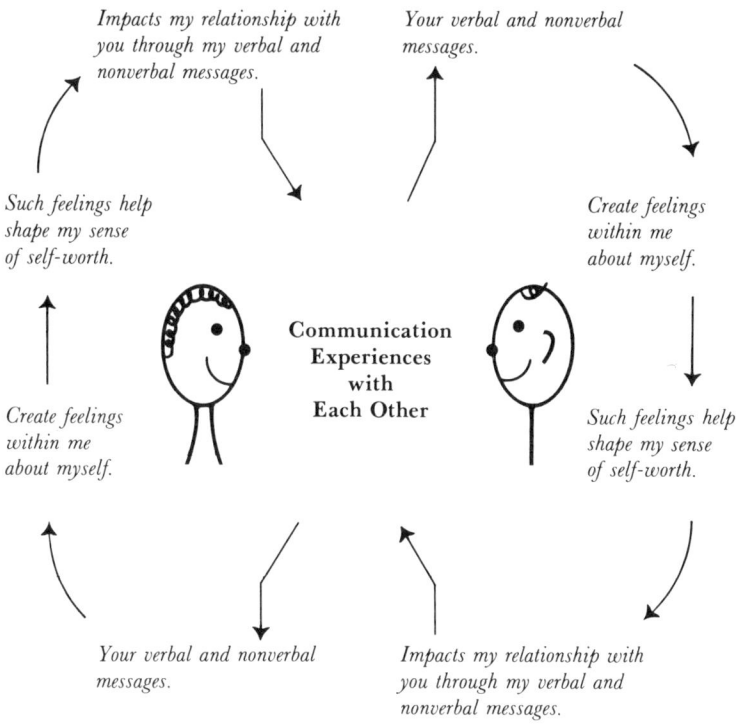

Figure 2 **Self-Esteem Formation**

The vocation of marriage invites us to be guardians of each other's self-esteem. It gives us the responsibility to regard the care and nurture of each other's self-worth as a sacred trust. As we affirm the self-worth of our spouse, we contribute to his or her personal well-being, capacity to reach out to others, and ability to trust God.

Critical to the enrichment of self-esteem in others is communication. Through both nonverbal and verbal communication, we show appreciation and affirm our spouse. The manner in which we speak and act can enhance the feelings of worth in the other. In the development of other themes in this book, we will discuss several communication behaviors that build self-esteem. We hope that the way these skills are esteem builders will become clear. They are very different from the behaviors listed at the beginning of this chapter, "A Plan Guaranteed to Ruin Your Marriage."

Being Mediators of God's Grace

Self-esteem is important to both effective marital living and to vital, trusting faith in God. As we guard and encourage each other's self-worth, we create within the other the capacity to respond to God's caring, affirming Word with deep, abiding trust. Our faith relationship to God often is blocked at the level of our self-worth: We find it difficult to believe God is caring and loving when we don't believe that about ourselves.

When we choose to love, affirm, and care for our partner with deep love, we become a mediator of the grace of God. Our love for our mate can potentially free a self-doubting partner to experience more concretely and affirm more deeply that God is love. Such an experience creates the feeling that, "I'm lovable because I've been loved by you and You." Faith is nurtured at its deepest roots when self-esteem is enriched.

EXERCISE

We live or die inside to the degree that we are appreciated and affirmed by our marriage partner. Use the following exercise to express appreciation to your spouse.

Instructions: Complete the statement, "I appreciate it when you," 10 or more times. Take time to write out your personal statements of appreciation. Study them. Then, read your list to your spouse. Afterward, discuss the results. Describe how you feel about being appreciated by your spouse.

Husband

I appreciate it when you

1. _____
2. _____
3. _____
4. _____
5. _____
6. _____
7. _____
8. _____
9. _____
10. _____
11. _____
12. _____
13. _____

Wife

I appreciate it when you

1. _____
2. _____
3. _____
4. _____
5. _____
6. _____
7. _____
8. _____
9. _____
10. _____
11. _____
12. _____
13. _____

MEDITATION

My spouse accepts me—
me, with my funny nose
and plump body.
That significant person
   in my life
accepts
the way I speak,
the way I act in private
   and in public—
the way I really am.

Because I am accepted,
I see more clearly who I am
and accept myself with zeal.

I have no desire
   to be another.

I am myself—simply
   and completely.
Love defines the person
I really am and will be.
And I am untroubled
   and unshamed
by this definition.

Please, God, never allow
   me to despair
because I am who I am.

CHAPTER 4

NURTURING FAITH THROUGH TALKING AND LISTENING

REFLECTION

God's story
My story
The Christian Story
A recital of Love's initiative and humanity's response.

The Christian story is a tale about faith. It's a record of a God who in many and different ways has communicated unconditional love to human beings in word and action. This self-disclosing, compassionate Divine Being desires a response to this initiative. The Christian story is a narrative about a trusting and mistrusting people in relationship to a faithful God.

This story is a historical chronicle, but it's also a contemporary, ongoing set of events. For the Jesus-story is "my, your, our" story. God's reaching out in Jesus Christ, and my personal response makes for a continuing dialogue of faith. The story continues as long as God initiates and I respond in faith to the divine action of love.

Every Christian has a faith story to share. Each in his or her own way responds to the narrative of God's love in Christ. Our faith is rooted in the variety of experiences that have occurred in our personal history. For these experiences to remain alive and to nurture our faith, they need to be told to others. And in order for our faith stories to be useful, they must be heard.

When talking and listening occur, we have dialogue. Such dialogue is important in Christian marriage. For it's through honest talk and careful listening that we discover ourselves, each other, and our God. Telling and listening to faith stories assists mutual faith discovery, mutual growth in faith, and spiritual intimacy.

Discovering One's Faith History

Myron: "I have often told Jan about the many hours of conversation I had with my dad in the living room in the evening, in the pickup truck enroute to installing TV aerials (Dad Chartier was in TV and radio sales and service), and in many other places. These conversations were about the nature of faith in God, about the way to Christian living, about Christian vocation, and other things. When I tell Jan about the important role my father played in nurturing my faith, I get in touch with the parental dynamics that were the well-springs of my trust in God."

Jan: "When I tell Myron about the role of the Bible in my upbringing, I discover some of the dynamics which nurtured my young faith in God. I tell him, for example, about memories of my elderly grandmother who read every day from a big family Bible. That book and that woman left an indelible impression upon me. When I was old enough to read, my mother had me read the Bible to her while she ironed. I read the Bible to my mother in this way until I was old enough to take on the task of ironing for the family. This weekly oral bible reading not only nurtured my mother's faith, but also gave me a knowledge of the Scriptures."

By being caring, responsive listeners to each other, we encourage and implicitly invite deep sharing of faith from one another. As each partner in a marital relationship shares and listens, a bridge of trust is constructed, which makes deeper self-revelation possible. The dialogue is a mutual exchange of listening and sharing activity. When we engage in such in-depth talk about personal faith, we gain personal and deeper insight into the dynamics of faith.

Discovering Current Faith Dynamics

To tell the *history* of our personal faith requires less risk than to reveal the *here-and-now* dynamics of our faith. Our contemporary stories involve risk, for there is less certainty about our trust relationship with God. We lack the historical perspective. As we verbalize to our spouse what we are thinking, feeling, and experiencing, we discover the current status of our trust relationship with God, and this is not always pleasant. Such here-and-now sharing of faith requires a trustworthy listener in the person of our spouse. To illustrate this point, we'd like to describe a situation from our own family.

In 1981 our son, Tim, became ill with a long-term viral infection of the inner ear and the cranial nerves. He complained of dizziness and weakness in his legs for three weeks. Doctors had trouble diagnosing what was wrong. Finally, we rushed him to the emergency room of Lankenau Hospital in Philadelphia where he spent a week. He was fed intravenously for three days. It was determined he had had a strong reaction to a viral infection and that his inner ear was involved.

Upon taking him home, we discovered he was unable to walk without support. During the next week, his ability to walk deteriorated. We called the doctor, which meant a trip to a pediatric neurologist. The diagnosis was vestibular neuronitis. The healing process would be very slow.

Four weeks later, Tim not only couldn't walk, but also was bothered by light and sound. His skin was actually sensitive to touch. He had trouble writing. Puzzled, the doctor sent him to Children's Hospital, where two days of tests revealed that Tim had no terrible death-threatening diseases. Still, he couldn't walk, he couldn't write, and he reacted negatively to light and sound. Weeks went by. Finally, two months later the illness seemed to have run its course, and Tim re-entered the hospital for recuperation therapy.

He responded slowly. Progress came by weeks rather than days. He was hospitalized for eight weeks. Since that time, Tim has continued to make progress, although not without some setbacks. At this writing, his recovery is almost complete, and he's able to live a fairly normal, active life.

For parents to live through the devastating illness of a child is to be confronted with a serious personal relational crisis. Dealing with the unknowns of a child's illness is a demanding experience, emotionally and spiritually. It requires all the resources one has and even more. Indeed, the question becomes "Will we/I survive this experience?"

Experience with long illness in a marriage or in a family creates a crisis of faith. Only when mates verbalize their struggles do they gain understanding into the deeper reality of what it means to trust in God. Granted, expressing these faith struggles is extremely difficult. Words seem so inadequate to describe the inner turmoil we undergo as we seek to find our faith anchor.

We (Jan and Myron) know. We've been there. Tim's illness created a crisis of faith for us. The crisis was different for each of us. But in the midst of our pain, exhaustion, frustration, anger, and fear we sought to express to each other where we were in our trust relationship with God. It was very important for us to verbalize these feelings so that we could understand how each other felt. We affirm John Powell's maxim that, "I must be able to *tell* you who I am before I can *know* who I am." Before I can really understand who I am before God, I must be able to reveal to you who I am. What is not verbalized or expressed remains vague, like a reality covered by fog or even worse, smog, until it's revealed in the clear daylight of another human being's presence.

Myron: "As Tim's father, I struggled with my life of prayer. I would say to Jan, 'What do I pray for? Do I pray for Tim to get well? What if he dies—does that mean God didn't care? Do I pray for Tim to get well soon, so he won't have to suffer so much and be away from his school friends so long? What does that kind of prayer mean when the illness has no end in sight? What is the meaning of illness in the world God created? For what do I have a right to pray? Speedy recovery? Full recovery? Divine healing? How do you pray and for what do you pray when you don't understand the illness, when the doctors know so little, and it drags on day after day, week after week, month after month, bill after bill? What if he should be an invalid for the rest of his life; how do you pray? What does it mean to trust God in a time when life seems to be falling apart?"

"Those questions in many ways were my questions (very lonely ones) before God. To verbalize them, to hear myself over a period of months disclose them to Jan, gave them a shared quality, gave me insight into my faith relationship with God. I'm not sure I'm any clearer today about how and what to pray in such difficult times. But I must pray because God is faithful in listening to the questions that haunt me when I'm alone and in the middle of the night. I discovered that praying is an act of faith. It is a declaration that God is present even when life's circumstances declare that he is absent. Prayer placed me in the arms of a trustworthy God. Of that I was sure."

Jan: "As Tim's mother, I struggled with God's purpose in the whole experience. I knew I would never find an answer to my asking 'Why?' I had asked that before in life and learned that a genuine, satisfying answer isn't there. I didn't want to pour energy into that question knowing full well I would probably reach the same conclusion. However, I did feel compelled to search for God's presence and purpose in it all: What was Tim supposed to be learning? What was all this suffering going to prove? When he prayed to get well, what was God's response? What was I to learn? All the lessons I could think of I had already walked through. I feared that anything that happened in my relationship with God would be for the worse and not the better. As months passed, I knew I didn't have sufficient strength to face each new day on my own. I wondered if God would sustain me. I asked similar questions about Myron as father and Melody as a sister, who was receiving far less attention than she deserved or needed.

"In various forms and structures, I struggled with these kinds of issues and questions. I occasionally shared these struggles with Myron. Through the sharing, I gained clarity on what it was I was really saying. I saw my struggle in new ways. In knowing that Myron had listened, I gained confidence that God, too, listened and understood. In spite of the struggles, my faith deepened."

Listening to contemporary stories of faith can be very demanding.

If a spouse is struggling with doubt or redefining the nature of personal faith, the other spouse may find it very threatening and move to a defensive listening posture. Such a position seeks to communicate to the other that their previous position was okay. There is no need for change. Such a position tries to cut off a person's discussion about their changing faith and the newfound richness in their trust relationship with God.

As we reveal our personal faith to others, we discover who we are as faithing persons. I need you to listen to me in all my certainties and in all my doubts. I need you, as my life partner, to understand me as I understand myself before God. As you listen, I discover my faith. I come to know myself through being known by you. The faith we express is the one we possess. To learn to listen in ways that facilitate faith discovery is one of the greatest gifts we can give each other as a couple.

Mutual Growth in Faith

Sharing the story of one's faith pilgrimage also facilitates personal growth. Self-disclosure is a primary ingredient for growth in faith. If I'm unwilling to share the story of my faith pilgrimage with my spouse, growth is likely to stop because self-understanding will be retarded. Many Christians have not progressed in faith development because they fail to verbalize their trust relationship with God. Their maturity level has not moved beyond that of a child. The maturation of one's personal faith is worked out by voluntarily disclosing larger and larger parts of one's faith experience and perspective with a trustworthy "other" like one's spouse.

By sharing my faith, I can gain insight into myself as a faithing, trusting person, and through the dialogue I can discover where growth in my God relationship is needed. Through this process of sharing and discovering, I can evaluate my faith development and make changes accordingly.

Myron: "Sharing the story of my faith struggle with Jan made me realize that deeper trust in God is required in difficult times than in less stressful ones. When the answers weren't clear and life was tense, I was tempted to demand from God clarity to life's dilemmas. What I was being asked was to trust God with abandonment. What I had previously known intellectually about the faithfulness of God through the stories of Abraham and Isaac and Job, I was now learning in an experiential way. In the stress of my life, I was learning, 'When life is difficult, trust the God who breathed into you the breath of life. Put your destiny into his control. Depend upon him.' "

Jan: "Although my concerns and struggles during Tim's illness seemed very different from Myron's, we discovered that I had reached many similar conclusions. I had experienced God's faithfulness in new depth, my trust had grown. As months pass, I now can see God's purposes in those experiences. God really was in it with us. I can affirm that with greater conviction and clarity."

Spiritual Intimacy

When we choose to talk about and listen to each other's faith stories, we enrich our marital relationship and experience spiritual intimacy. The more we share, the deeper will be our spiritual intimacy. A relational bond of trust and intimacy is formed. This process of sharing and listening builds a relationship of faith, hope, and love.

A relationship of faith materializes because our personal stories of faith are openly exchanged. The strengths and vulnerabilities of our trust relationship with God are explored. We consider together how faith was formed, nurtured, challenged, and acted upon.

A relationship of hope is created because, by sharing our stories, we see the reality of God embodied in our personal experiences. As long as we have stories of faith to reveal to each other, there is hope. As long as we can remind each other of God's steadfast love and faithfulness at work in our personal lives and in our marriage, there is every reason to move into the future with confidence, knowing there will be new stories of faith to share and to listen to.

A relationship of love forms because the telling and hearing of faith stories create closeness, spiritual intimacy.

> Our faith pilgrimage—
> its victories and its failures,
> its beauty and its deformity,
> its depth and its shallowness,
> its wisdom and its folly,
> its joy and its pain,
> its hope and its despair—
> draws us together.

As we hear about each other's spiritual formation, about struggles of faith, about personal crises, about special people of faith in our lives, we gain an appreciation for our spouse as a child of God. In listening to our spouse's story of faith, we are invited to walk around the story, discover our own place, and remain in it. The experiences related may confront us but they don't oppress. They will inspire but not manipulate. Indeed, they invite us as husband and wife to mutual encounter, dialogue, sharing. They create a relational bond of love — a spiritual intimacy.

This exchange is a circular process: persons of faith create a marital relationship of faith which in turn brings forth "faithing" persons. Our sharing creates spiritual intimacy which, in turn, nurtures the faith within each of us.

Beginning the Process

In this discussion, we (Myron and Jan) have tried to help you see that talking and listening are of vital importance in a marriage. Specifically, talking about and listening to stories of faith leads to growth and intimacy. We want to motivate you to share with each other in new and deeper ways. However, we want to forewarn you that such sharing may be very difficult for some. Faith is a personal matter. Talking about faith is risky. We may feel a loss for words. We may fear that our faith stories will be ridiculed, misunderstood, ignored, or rejected by the one we love. We may experience feelings of inadequacy. To deal with these feelings requires considerable effort. The first step is to begin. The beginning may be quite small. That's a start. It can grow from there.

Sharing with Others

Once we have engaged in faith dialogue within our marriage, we may realize that our faith stories need to be told and heard in the larger community of faith, the church. The whole church can benefit from the faith pilgrimages of God's children. However, it's unlikely that our sharing will be genuine or life-changing unless it occurs in the primary relationships of our lives — in marriage and in family. Deep sharing requires trustworthy relationships. Such relationships are built and nurtured on self-disclosing communication. Our marriages are a beginning point.

EXERCISE

Instructions: Below you will find two horizontal lines. The dot at the left represents the *beginning point* in your faith development. The dot at the right represents *the present point* in your life and spiritual formation. The lines represent your faith life and its development.

Take time to reflect upon your faith life from its beginning until now: Who have been the important people in your faith formation — in the past and presently? Who has helped the development of your trust relationship with God in Jesus Christ?

For each significant person, draw a vertical line through the horizontal line at the appropriate place in your faith development history. Above the vertical line place that person's initials.

After you have drawn your faith time-line, consider the impact each person has had upon you. What was special about her/him as a person? What was unique about his/her faith? How did he/she nurture your relationship with God? Make some notes about each person in response to these questions.

After you have each completed your task, discuss together the results of your exploration. Be sure to share insights gained about your faith development.

Husband

B   P

Notes:

Wife

B   P

Notes:

MEDITATION

"No one can develop freely in this world and find a full life without feeling understood by at least one person. No one comes to know himself through introspection, or in the solitude of his personal diary. Rather it is in dialogue, in his meeting with other persons."

Paul Tournier

O Lord of my faith, give me ears to hear my spouse's story of learning to trust in you. Provide me with clear speech to tell my story of being related to you. May we both grow as faithing persons through our dialogue. Amen.

CHAPTER 5

NURTURING FAITH THROUGH CENTRICITY

REFLECTION

A Monologue

"How important am I to you? That's a crucial question, my spouse. Am I central to your life? I need to hear your words. More than your words, I need to see you live out my importance in your life. I need to know I count. Sometimes you seem so busy, or preoccupied, or wrapped up in other persons, I wonder if I really do count with you. Sometimes I find myself asking: 'Do I count to my spouse? Do I *really* count?' These questions scare me when they fly through my mind. Sometimes I struggle to block them out. As I think about it, it's not the questions that frighten me. It's your response . . . your answer. I'm not clear what you would say if I asked my questions to you directly. Are you aware I try to find out how central I am? I watch you. I listen to you. I even ask you to do little or even big things. It's not so much the things that need doing. I could do them myself. Many of them don't have to be done. The issue is so much deeper. I'm asking you to do it for me . . . because I'm important. When you do it, I feel good. You don't always pull through. Then I wonder: Why? If I would have asked for something else, would you have done it? Do I not count with you? How do I know?

"When we were dating, I *knew* I counted in your life. In fact, it seemed that no one and no thing came even close to my importance to you. I was the center of your world. You were the center of mine. We were in 'our world' together. We were central to each other. I went out of my way to let you hear my message: 'You are central. There is absolutely no question that you count.' I heard the same message from you. I'm sure I did. It resounded around me. I felt secure and safe. I thought it would last forever.

"I remember our wedding. We promised. We pledged to keep each other central. I believed we would do that . . . I thought it would be forever—you at the center of my life—I at the center of yours.

"When did I begin to wonder? Maybe I wondered before we were married, but I couldn't look at it then. I can hardly look at it now. There were so many things: my job, your job, your mother's illness, having the babies, buying our home, moving, my dad's death, getting money in the bank. We just kept going, assuming we were important and central to each other. Somewhere along the line I began to ask: 'Where am I with you in all of this? Where are you with me?' The answers weren't easy.

"I was coming to bed an hour later than you. You had quit bugging me about it. You wanted me to go out to dinner with 'just you.' I chose to go with my group. I thought you and I could have dinner another time. Then I saw your hurt. But when I wanted you to attend the symphony when we were given tickets, you were too tired. I asked a friend. One year I forgot your birthday and had to get a cake and a gift at the last minute. You were out of town for mine.

"It seems that I have moved to the outer edge of what's important to you! Maybe it only appears that way. But I wonder . . . I really do wonder . . . Am I wrong? Could I be right? It's a crucial question, my spouse. If I asked you, what answer would you give?"

* * * * *

Centricity is the issue of this monologue. Centricity is at the heart of every intimate relationship. What is it? It's the degree of priority one holds in the life of another. It's defined by the crucial questions: How important am I to you? How central am I? How much do I count? How often, when, and under what circumstances do I come first—before anything else—in your life? Furthermore, centricity involves the responses to these questions by the other.

When a couple chooses to say "Yes" to each other in marriage, they indicate that the other has become the first and most intimate person in their life. The traditional wedding vows bind them together through better times and worse times, through vibrant health and disabling sickness, through all of life with its ups and downs—until death parts them. During the period of the engagement, the wedding, and the early months of marriage, many couples feel surrounded by something akin to an invisible romantic halo. They have no doubt that each is central to the other and that it "forevermore will be so."

But bothersome tasks to be done, awesome decisions to be made, regrettable mistakes not to be undone—these and other things begin to tarnish the romantic halo of safety and security. One spouse or the other, or even both at once, may realize that so much energy has gone into convincing the other of his or her centricity that some personal needs and preferences have been neglected. So there may be a backing away . . . at least enough so that each can be comfortable. The issues are different from relationship to relationship, but the balancing of "your centrality with the way I live my life" begins to occur. The couple somewhere face the reality that the total attention of a *you-count* stance which marked the early commitment period is now modified by the essential phrase *but I count, too.* Balance is important for a healthy rewarding marriage relationship. However, it often must be accomplished in very hurtful ways which create doubt and suspicion rather than deeper love and understanding.

What happens? How can we gain insight? What can we do? There is no simple answer or formula which fits all persons. But the following thoughts about centricity in a marriage relationship may provide some insight.

Centricity Involves Choice

"When I chose to marry my spouse, I chose *not* to marry someone else who could have been a potential intimate." Couples make a choice to be for each other, a choice of togetherness and oneness in that specific relationship. Some couples seem to believe that once the choice is made, it lasts forever with little, if any, conscious attention. Unfortunately, choices of this depth and magnitude require careful monitoring and nurturing. They have to be renewed, reshaped, and remade as the relationship changes.

Each spouse meets new people, becomes challenged in new ways, faces new demands and responsibilities. In the midst of all this newness, it's easy to forget that the commitment to centricity is still as important as ever. When this commitment is neglected, each spouse is left to wonder, "Am I still central? Perhaps there is someone or something else."

Centricity in Marriage Requires Mutuality

"If you are central in my life, then it's important that I am central in yours, too." One of the joys and rewards of keeping another person central in one's life is the assurance of knowing that the other's commitment is similar. Such mutuality is a sustaining factor through all of life's happenings.

In the mix of responsibilities demanded by marriage and family living, centricity may be taken for granted. A working spouse gives an increasing amount of time toward advancement in position and pay. The parent invests much energy in meeting the needs of the newly arrived infant. The energy, time, and money invested in recreational activities or in maintaining a recently purchased home involve both persons. Whatever the cause, a couple may discover that the numerous ways by which they once demonstrated the other's centricity have nearly disappeared from their patterns of being together in life. When spouses realize that there is no recognition of or response to what they have invested and lived out, discouragement follows. Feelings will surface which may lead eventually to seeking someone or something which will offer reward and repayment.

Counselors repeatedly tell of experiences in marriage counseling when one spouse accuses the other of not caring. The conversation may sound something like this:

> She: "He just doesn't care about me any more."
> He: (looking surprised) "What do you mean 'I don't care?' "
> She: "You don't. Everything else comes first. I'm a tag-a-long in your life."
> He: (looking shocked) "Wait a minute. I care. I work long hours. I repair the house. I do a million other things. Maybe I am too busy, but most of it I do for you and the kids. If you think I do it all for myself, you've got to be crazy. No way."
> She: (looking skeptical) "Well, why don't you say so once in a while?"
> He: "Why should I have to?"
> She: "Did it ever cross your mind that we—the kids and especially I—would rather have your love some other way? Why does it all have to be *your* way?"

This illustrative conversation points out at least two more aspects of centricity. First, centricity will be more meaningful in a marriage if it is clearly communicated. Second, how centricity is lived out and expressed involves the expectations and needs of both persons. Therefore, the way in which centricity is expressed must be negotiated. The people we are most likely to take for granted are family members and friends close to us. We get so involved and pressed by demands in living our lives that we assume the persons crucial to our well-being will know of our love and care. We forget to speak the affirming words or fail to do the little things that once told these persons they were important to us. We forget that at least a portion of our reasons for doing what we are now doing is rooted in our commitment to them.

Partners in a marriage need regularly to hear from each other, "You are the central person in my life." Such a message may be sent from one spouse to another in small ways—a flower, a lunch out, a movie, a carefully selected card. Each spouse tells the other in a chosen way, "I care about you. You count."

The impact may not be the one intended by the mate. The flower was picked up at the local stop-and-go market—not the flower shop as in the "old" days—and the recipient may interpret this as "less love."

So, negotiation becomes important. If I'm clearly told by my mate that I'm important and assured of that by certain behavior, it helps me to feel I *count*. Sometimes, though, I need the opportunity to tell you what would mean more. I might want to say: "Hey, don't bring the flower this time; take an extra fifteen minutes to hold me in your arms. I need that!" How centricity is expressed in a relationship requires ongoing communication and mutual negotiation. It demands investment of personhood.

Centricity Involves Overcoming Barriers and Hurdles

Committing oneself to the holding of another person as central in your life can be fearsome. It raises many questions: What if the other makes so many demands that I can't meet them? Am I worthy of being in this kind of relationship? Can I do my part? What happens if I don't?

Every marriage relationship involves disappointments. There are moments of anger and intense conflict in regard to values and goals. We feel hurt and lonely when our mate fails to be empathic toward our needs, whether they be minor or major. We feel betrayed when promises made aren't kept. As relational hurt and pain creep into a marriage, partners may discover that centricity is at stake unless these negative factors are faced and worked through. To maintain the centricity of one to the other in a relationship, genuine forgiveness is required.

But forgiveness is much more than good intentions to do better. Indeed, it's the capacity to turn back and face our mate. With courage, we face whatever injuries have occurred and their consequences. We take whatever action is necessary to rework and repair the hurts, pains, and injuries. Forgiving actions by couples are deep reaffirmations of centricity.

How Does Centricity Relate to Our Faith?

The first and greatest commandment is that we, as God's children, should love the Lord with all our hearts, our souls, our minds, and our strength (Lk 10:27). That is a commandment of centricity in no uncertain terms. God is to be "Number One" in our lives. No questions, no negotiation. This is the only way we find wholeness and freedom as human beings.

But the second commandment is like it. That commandment is to love our neighbor as we love ourselves (Mt 22:39). Throughout Scripture, we find that if we love and are obedient to God, then it follows that we will choose to live in right relationships with other persons. Our closest neighbor is the spouse whom we have chosen and have bound ourselves to. To live faithfully and loyally within that relationship is a requirement, as well as an outflow of our love of God. Committing oneself to hold another person central is part of Christian discipleship. Love of and obedience to God and loving, life-giving relationships with other persons are at the very heart and core of Christian faith.

In Christian marriage, the centricity of my spouse can't come before the centralness of God. To replace love for God with love for spouse is to commit an act of idolatry. On the other hand, my life partner's centricity is the most significant human relationship I have over time. Consequently, my love for and obedience to God is closely interwoven with the centricity of my spouse. It's important to see that the two are complementary, not contradictory. God is the center for us both. He's present in the betweenness that makes our relationship unique.

We often fail in our broken and limited humanity to keep God central. So, too, we struggle with centricity in marriage. We commit ourselves before God and the Christian community to keeping each other central. But inevitably, we discover that the task of following through on that commitment is more difficult than we imagined. Our humanness gets in the way. The push and pull of other priorities is strong — our jobs, our relationships with other people, our drive to be fulfilled and successful. Our intention is good, but following through is another matter.

In marriage, our humanity is quite apparent. After a day of pouring out energies into other persons' lives with intensity and grace, we reunite with our spouse spent and exhausted, with no grace left. We want to do better. Our intention is to be kind and loving. But our mean, cross, impatient side emerges. We feel our human limitations. And although we yearn to be different — to spend more energy, to be more patient, to have more control — we experience ourselves as failures. Shame and guilt emerge and run high.

Our faith speaks a word of hope to us in these moments of despair. Repeatedly, Israel moved away from God and his way. However, God was always present, ready to forgive and to allow his people to begin anew. God reached out to Israel, renewing them with the strength of his grace.

As persons of faith, we have the power to accept our limitations, own our failures, ask for forgiveness, and work for new beginnings. As married couples, we can be sources of strength for each other, learning from our failures, renewing our covenants, and continuing to move on in hope.

* * * * *

The question of centricity in marriage is similar to that affecting our relationship to God: We lose perspective on our priorities; we affirm our faith verbally but fail to act upon it; we expend our energy before we've given ample time or thought to that central other. Our intentions are good, but our performance is poor.

One of the great challenges of marriage is to hold ourself and our spouse accountable to these commitments of centricity. With steady investment, persons will grow, relationships will thrive, and faith will deepen. All three are intricately interrelated.

EXERCISE

Instructions: Below is a series of statements. Complete them without the assistance of your spouse. After each of you has completed the open-ended sentences, exchange responses and discuss your answers.

Wife

1. Some reasons I chose to make you central in my life are:

2. Some ways I have tried to show you that you count with me are:

3. Some ways I believe you have assured me that I count to you are:

4. Some hurdles we have faced in keeping each other central are:

5. Some of the human limitations I experience in trying to keep you central are:

6. Some new beginnings I would like to make in expressing your importance to me are:

Husband

1. Some reasons I chose to make you central in my life are:

2. Some ways I have tried to show you that you count with me are:

3. Some ways I believe you have assured me that I count to you are:

4. Some hurdles we have faced in keeping each other central are:

5. Some of the human limitations I experience in trying to keep you central are:

6. Some new beginnings I would like to make in expressing your importance to me are:

MEDITATION

REMEMBERING

I remember, Lord, when I first committed my life to you by making you central.

I remember when I renewed that commitment to your lordship.

I remember the growing relationship with my spouse as we moved toward centricity.

I remember our struggle to keep faith with that commitment.

QUESTIONING

Where am I right now in my commitment to keep you central, to acknowledge you as the Lord of all my life?

Where am I now in my commitment to keep my spouse central?

How do I see my partner's commitment to keep me central?

COMMITTING

My commitment to you and to my life partner:
O God, in light of the past and the answers to my present questions, I am prepared to make the following commitments:

Thank you for loving me and providing the opportunity to renew old covenants and make new beginnings. Be present in these commitments and in our oneness. Amen.

CHAPTER 6

NURTURING FAITH THROUGH CARING

REFLECTION

Imagine yourself coming home some evening. As you approach the door, you see a poster tacked upon it with these words:

WANTED
A Caring Spouse

REWARD
A Satisfying, Long-Term Marriage

As you enter the house, you ask: "Hey, what's this poster all about?" Your spouse responds, "Sometimes I wonder if you care about me. Are you really a caring spouse?"

Caring—An Indispensable Ingredient

Caring is an indispensable ingredient of a satisfying marriage. Indeed, it's a primary nutrient for anyone growing in relationship to others and to God. The significance of caring in marriage was documented in a study published in 1980 by Floyd and Harriett Thatcher entitled, *Long-Term Marriage: A Search for the Ingredients of a Lifetime Partnership*. The Thatchers came up with five characteristics needed for a satisfying marriage relationship, one of which was *caring*.

How did they define *caring* in this study? "It is wanting the other person, husband or wife, to have room to grow and develop and express his or her own personhood without feeling threatened or left out. Caring is wanting the best for the other person, not trying to score at the expense of our partner—building up the other person, setting the stage and creating the environment for a full expression of his or her capabilities.

"Caring, by this definition, does not involve two people going their separate ways in pursuit of individual goals without thought of the other's feelings. But it does leave room for the other person to engage in satisfying activities with reassuring feelings of support rather than destructive feelings of being in competition. And caring makes it possible for two distinctly different individuals to live in a life-style of

---

*The material in this chapter is based partially upon the thinking of Milton Mayeroff in *On Caring,* New York, NY, Harper and Row, 1971 and David Augsburger in *Caring Enough to Hear and Be Heard,* Ventura, Ca., Regal Books, 1982.

closeness and intimacy without becoming victims of flypaper love and marriage" (p. 196). To care for one's life partner is at the center of married life.

Caring—Its Essence

Caring is an essential thread in the fabric of marriage. To care for one's spouse is to invite the growth and realization of his/her full human potential. Caring is an invitation to growth that educes the best from one's partner. Motivated by those desires that will complete, mature, and fulfill the other, caring is an active labor of love. It's the opposite of simply using the other person to satisfy one's own needs. As a process, caring is a way of relating to one's spouse that involves his/her growth and development as a creature of God.

The essence of caring in marriage can be stated through a series of contrasting but related statements.

In caring,
I perceive my spouse as similar to myself,
as an extension of myself,
as continuous with myself.

Furthermore, in caring,
I perceive my spouse as different from myself,
as separate from myself,
as unique from myself.

As husband and wife, we are very much alike. We experience the same basic human needs for physical well-being, safety and security, love and belonging, self-esteem and a sense of being valued, purpose and meaning in life. We are similar, we are not foreigners to each other.

But we are also very different. I roll the toothpaste tube; you squeeze it. I go to bed early; you are a night owl. You are mechanically inclined; I'm a klutz. You are you; I am me. Nothing in us is identical. Each of us is unique and special, one of a kind, a gift to the other.

I experience you as an extension of myself; at the same time, I experience you as separate from me, having worth and value in your own right. I have no need to dominate and control you, to possess and exploit you to satisfy my personal needs and ambitions. I don't *own* you. I care for you, your uniqueness, and your individuality. Because I care, I have no desire to manipulate you to fulfill myself or to crush your personhood in achieving my goals. I value and care for you as *you*. And in valuing you, I value myself.

In caring,
I appreciate and encourage the growth potential of my spouse.
I invite my mate
to respond to his/her need
to grow and develop.

Furthermore, in caring,
I am delighted with my spouse's growth
in his/her intrinsic way.
By responding
to inherent growth needs,
my mate discovers and realizes selfhood
as he/she becomes what God intended.

To care for you is to help you grow, to facilitate your becoming all that God created you to be. By caring, I bid you to grow. I challenge you to discover your growth needs, to reach out and become all you can be. I will attempt to help you without violating your freedom, dignity, or self-responsibility. I desire that you experience the fullness of your humanity as one of God's creatures.

As you discover your inner needs and grow, I am delighted. For in growing, you discover and become your true self. And in caring about you, I cherish your growth as a person in your own right. That growth may frighten me as it takes turns I'm unprepared for, but the act of caring for you will provide the security I need.

In caring,
I experience my mate as needing me
in order to grow.
I experience my spouse's well-being
as connected to my own.

Furthermore, in caring,
I seek my mate's development
as an autonomous, responsible being.
I cannot grow
on my spouse's behalf.

As you fulfill your need to grow, I experience you as needing me in order for that process to occur. This doesn't mean that only I, as your spouse, can satisfy your needs. Your need for me doesn't permit me to dominate you. Rather, your growth has been entrusted to me, as has my growth been entrusted to you. When we spoke our marriage vows, I was entrusted with your care and you with mine. Now, my well-being is bound up with yours. As you grow, my own welfare is enhanced.

And yet, your worth as my partner goes beyond your ability to meet my needs. You're a person in your own right — an independent, responsible being. Your growth comes from within you; it isn't dependent upon me. I can't grow for you. Growth must come from within each of us personally.

In caring,
I am available to direct growth,
to point the way to maturity and wholeness.
I don't dominate or manipulate
but suggest and stimulate.

Furthermore, in caring,
I don't impose my own direction;
rather, I respect the growth needs of my spouse
and am guided by those needs.

Caring for you involves presence and dialogue. Through these, I come close to you without violating your worth, freedom, and personal responsibility. In closing the personal distance, we touch. I hear the beats of your desire for life, your drive toward self-fulfillment, your deep yearning for intimacy, your need to be esteemed as a separate person, your accountability to yourself and to the important persons in your life.

As I listen to you, I become more sensitive to you, remaining silent as you make decisions freely and responsibly, trusting that wisdom you possess will direct you in your next steps, whether they be painful or joyful.

Through my presence to you, and from our dialogue, I try to enable your becoming. I seek to direct or guide your growth without domination, imposition, or manipulation. My caring direction is guided by my sensitivity to your needs. It is your welfare alone that I seek.

*In caring,
I don't help my partner grow
in order to fulfill and actualize myself.
My spouse is never a means to my end.*

*Furthermore, in caring,
as I summon my spouse to grow,
I do fulfill and actualize myself.
Treating my mate as a separate other
becomes my means to wholeness.*

My caring for you need not be rewarded in my own growth. You are valued as a person with your own integrity; you are not a channel for my ends.

Nevertheless, in caring about your growth *I* am fulfilled, *I* mature, *I* grow. *I* become whole in treating you as a person of great worth and value.

*In caring,
I show devotion to the growth and well-being of my spouse.
I commit myself to this person
and an unforeseeable
future with him/her.*

*Furthermore, in caring,
I am not burdened
by some outside force.
Rather, my devotion is a response to the value I see
in my marriage partner.*

Caring means devotion. It is through devotion that my care for you takes on substance and its own particular character. To care is to be committed for an unpredictable future. My caring devotion to you involves persistence, consistency, and generous giving even when difficulties would tempt me to hold back or to give up.

Devotedness isn't a burden. It isn't imposed by divine command or by your insistence. Rather, it's grounded in the value I see and experience in my interactions with you. It involves my total being, not simply the intellectual or emotional side of me. What I feel called to be to you, and what I want to do, come together in my caring for you. Rather than a burden, my devotion for you is a liberating experience.

*As I care, I grow.
I am fulfilled in my relationship
with my mate.
Caring is our vocation
as married persons,
our true nature as children of God.*

*Furthermore, as I care,
I bid my spouse to care.
He/she is fulfilled as a person
in caring.
He/she becomes responsive
to his/her need
to care.
As husband and wife,
we become partners
in this exchange.*

The success of a Christian marriage is measured by the extent of our care for each other. Care is our vocation. As I care for you, I grow and mature and bid you to fulfill your growth potential. As you care, you grow and mature, and invite me to fulfill my growth potential. In marriage, care is a mutual exchange. It fulfills our nature as persons created in God's image.

*Care, then, is
devotion
to the significant other in my life.*

*Furthermore, care gives my spouse
freedom to develop.*

Care: Its Principal Ingredients

Our care for each other is expressed through knowledge, patience, honesty, trust, humility, hope, and courage.

Knowledge

Caring involves more than good intentions or warm feelings. It demands that I understand my mate's needs and be able to respond appropriately to them.

Caring knowledge is quite different from our academic ways of discernment. The Western World has been highly influenced by Greek philosophy, which maintains that we "know" something only insofar as we are detached from it. The human task, from the Greek perspective, is to collect information about a person or object "out there," existing apart from ourselves. To become attached or emotionally involved with what is to be known is to distort our knowledge and prevent our ever knowing it.

Such cold detachment would undermine a marriage relationship. Caring knowledge of my spouse requires a dialogical relationship. Such relational knowledge guides my response to my partner's growth needs. An important skill in getting to know my mate is empathic listening. I seek to understand my partner not in part, but as a whole person with many interrelated parts. Marital partners attempt to know one another as they know themselves. Such relational knowledge keeps the act of caring from being sentimental about and/or blind to the needs of the other.

Patience

The spouse who cares is patient. He/she is confident of the partner's growth potential. Growth can't be forced. It's nurtured by providing time to and for the other. If I'm impatient, I fail to give time, and I also take time away from my mate.

Growth is nurtured also by giving my spouse space. By empathic listening, by being present to my partner, I provide space for him or her to think, feel, do, become, and be. In short, the patient marriage partner gives the other room to live. I enlarge my spouse's living space rather than narrow it.

Besides being patient with my spouse, I must be patient with myself. I must give myself an opportunity to perceive, to discover, and to learn about both my mate and myself. Indeed, I must permit myself to care.

Honesty

Honesty is integral to caring. Honesty in relating to my mate involves two behavioral dynamics.

The first is an *accurate perception* of myself and my marriage partner. I must be honest with myself. I must know myself as I really am. Are my responses to my spouse's needs a help or a hindrance to growth? Can I identify when my good intentions are not helpful to my partner? When they aren't, am I able to make the appropriate adjustment?

To care, I must see others as they are, not as I would like them to be. To facilitate my spouse's growth, I must respond to his or her emerging needs. To idolize my spouse on the basis of the past or through illusions about the future militates against caring. I cannot allow a distorted view of my partner or myself.

The second behavioral dynamic involves what Carl R. Rogers calls *"congruence."* There must be no significant gap between what I say and how I act, between words and emotions. Authenticity assists the act of caring; pretense interferes with it.

Trust

Caring also involves trust—allowing the spouse to grow in his or her own way and time. To manipulate or force my mate into a mold shows a lack of trust on my part. I must entrust my mate to his/her own growth processes and the Spirit of God.

Most importantly, I must trust my own ability to care. If I constantly doubt my capacity to be present to my spouse, then I clearly lack trust in myself. And by focusing on this self-doubt, I become even more indifferent towards my spouse.

Humility

As I care for my spouse, I learn. Responsiveness to my partner involves continuous learning about him or her. I must be ready and willing to learn more about my marriage partner and myself. If I am beyond this, I can't be a caring person. The arrogant spouse isn't a caring spouse, for caring requires humility.

Hope

We hope that we will grow through our mutual caring. But my hope doesn't imply my mate's insufficiency. Rather, it expresses a present alive with possibilities which call us into the future. Indeed, hope rallies my energy and activates my strengths. It does not mean passively waiting for something to happen. We hope that both our spouse and our relationship together will grow through our mutual care.

One concrete way of expressing a caring hope is to pray for my life companion. Prayer affirms that our growth rests within the power of the Creative Spirit. No maturation is possible apart from this life force within us. When alone with God in prayer and silent meditation, we should always express hopeful care for the partner we love in marriage.

Courage

Caring is not easy. To care calls for courage because it involves the unknown. I can't predict or anticipate who or what my partner will become, or who I will become. And so, courage is needed. Yet, courage does not fly blind. It is supported by insights from the past and is built up by its openness to the present. "Trust in the other's ability to grow," says Milton Mayeroff, "and in my own ability to care gives me courage to go into the unknown, but it is also true that without the courage to go into the unknown such trust would be impossible."

Caring—Its Relationship to Faith

Caring is an essential thread in the fabric of the spiritual life. Besides being a primary nutrient in faith development, it is a way of participating in God's redeeming activity.

A Nutrient for a Growing Faith Relationship

Caring is essential in the nurturing of a deep, strong, trusting relationship with the living God. For you and me, this faith is developed, sustained, nurtured, and deepened within the context of a caring marriage, where the One who lets all things be releases his creative, transforming Spirit to empower our continuing growth.

Marriage is a relationship centered in Jesus, the human being for others. He is the model of all human maturity. As Christians, we know that God leads us through Christ. We base our lives and our marriage upon this conviction. Consequently, we choose to live a life of care rather than despair. Within our marriage, we care for each other both in times of growth and in times of crisis. To each other we say "You matter to me. I care deeply about your well-being." We act in such a way as to further each other's best interests and to promote each other's growth. We discover the presence of Jesus in this dialogue, this caring, this accepting, supportive concern that we extend to one another. When misunderstandings arise, and when hurt, loss, and death occur, we believe in and hope for another chance, a new beginning, life's power over death's grip. When caring is carried out in such a way, marriage companions experience an ever-growing maturity in Jesus Christ.

A Way of Participating in God's Redeeming Activity

A marriage distinguished by a caring attitude becomes a tiny colony of God in the midst of a secular world. But it isn't a refuge or fortress. Rather, it is a seedbed which enables each spouse to nurture faith and to respond to God's care as shown in Jesus Christ. A caring couple responds to the creative healing and renewing energies of the Spirit, and is able to turn outward to church and community in responsible, caring ways.

As couples become caring persons—to each other and to others—they point beyond themselves to a greater reality.

Henry J. M. Nouwen expressed this eloquently in a speech he gave in 1975 in Atlantic City: "To care . . . is not only the most human of all human acts, but also divine in nature, since by caring we participate intimately in God's redemptive work." As caring companions, we need to remind ourselves constantly that whatever growth occurs, whatever good happens, it's God's work and not our own.

EXERCISE

Instructions for the Wife
On this page, write a letter to your husband telling him your most personal thoughts and feelings about how you care for him. When you are done, show your letter to your husband and talk about it.

Instructions for the Husband
On this page, write a letter to your wife telling her your most personal thoughts and feelings about how you care for her. When you are done, show your letter to your wife and talk about it.

MEDITATION

"The more deeply I understand the central role of caring in my life, the more I realize it to be central to the human condition."

Milton Mayeroff

O God, you have shown me how to care through the example of your Son, Jesus Christ. Help me, now, to care for my spouse. Grant me wisdom, patience, honesty, trustworthiness, humility, hope, and courage. May I always be aware of and trust your caring presence in my life and in our marriage. In the name of the Good Shepherd. Amen.

CHAPTER 7

NURTURING FAITH THROUGH MUTUAL TRUST

REFLECTION

I trust you . . .
    I trust you not . . .
        I trust you . . .
            I trust you not . . .
                I TRUST YOU!

"I trust you! I *have* to trust you. We're getting married soon. Do you realize what that means? My well-being is in your hands for the rest of my life. You could, more than any other person, hurt and destroy me, even bring fatal damage to my faith relationship with God. But you love me. I love you. I *know* you won't bring me unnecessary pain. I trust you."

Trust: A Basic Ingredient

In conversations we've had with couples engaged to be married, this trust-you, trust-you-not vacillation has consumed much time and energy of the partners. As the wedding approaches, trust is usually very high: "I trust you. I know you love me, care for me, and respect me, and will continue to do so for the rest of our lives. I know you won't hurt me, attack me, abuse me, or be disloyal to me. You love me too much to do that. Because you are for me, it's with good reason that I trust you."

Mr. James Hine, a professional marriage counselor, researcher, and professor, has studied a number of successful marriages in depth (James R. Hine, *What Comes After You Say, "I Love You"?* Palo Alto: Pacific Books, 1980). The marriages were composed of couples whose love had deepened over years and whose relationship was strong. The couples listed reasons why they felt their marriages were successful. A number of characteristics emerged. First and foremost was trust in each other. Secondly, they had mutual respect. Third, they had been faithful and loyal in that relationship.

Trust really can't exist without mutual respect and fidelity. If we want our marriage relationships to deepen in love and to grow stronger, we must work at trusting and being trustworthy. Indeed mutual trust of each other is essential to a healthy, rewarding, satisfying marriage. It is also fertile ground for nurturing a vibrant trust relationship with God.

It's not surprising that trust is so crucial to a marriage relationship. Nothing significant can happen in any relationship unless the individuals involved trust each other. Trust must be present for growth and development.

Couples who feel good about their marriages often mention trust as a basic element. Why is trust so crucial? Because fear of being rejected, hurt, and betrayed falls away in a trusting relationship. Trust convinces me of acceptance, support, and love. Without trust, I live constantly with the fear of rejection by my spouse. With it, I'm confident that my spouse will build me up.

Characteristics of Trust

Trust is a word commonly used and everyone knows something of its meaning. Yet, it is a complex idea and hard to describe with words. To understand it better can help a marriage. Let's try to understand it by considering its characteristics.

1. *Trust involves risk.* My decision to trust can lead to either good or bad consequences. Marriage surely entails this kind of risk. To entrust my well-being to another makes me very vulnerable. It lowers my defenses. I can be easily and painfully hurt.

2. *The consequences of trust depend on the response of the other.* How will my mate respond to my entrustment of my self to him/her? I rely on my partner to accept rather than to reject me; to build me up rather than tear me apart; to support rather than ridicule me; to keep close to me rather than abandon me; to send me affirming messages rather than verbally attack me; to touch me with care rather than abuse me; to love me rather than ignore me. My spouse's response makes the difference.

3. *If the response is negative, I will be seriously hurt and scarred.* If I haven't invested a significant amount of trust in another, it's difficult for the other to inflict serious pain, apart from physical abuse. But if I have trusted another and that trust is betrayed, the personal and relational pain runs deep. In marriage, my partner can readily bring pain into my life. It takes little for me to feel that my trust has been betrayed.

4. *Trust develops as the other treats me with acceptance and support.* I'm not likely to trust a person whom I believe will treat me in ways which are hurtful. One reason trust is so deep at the time of marriage is that I simply can't believe my spouse will ever intentionally hurt me. My trust is implicit. I have great confidence in our future together and of my own well-being in the relationship.

5. *Trust grows slowly.* It's built step-by-step, bit-by-bit, beginning in the dating years. I feel attracted to the other. Slowly, I begin to trust. I share something of who I am, then I wait to see how the other will respond. If it's accepted and treated with respect and care, I'm ready to share and trust a bit more. The process is a slow one.

6. *Trust requires mutuality.* Trust grows slowly, and it deepens as each person demonstrates involvement in the process. After I have shared a significant part of myself with another, I wait for a response from them which shows they are willing to trust me. If the other person seems unwilling or unable to share him- or herself with me, I begin to wonder. Am I untrustworthy? Do I count? Is there someone else? Maybe the other is hiding something? Perhaps I am foolish to trust them. The questions go on. A trusting act received from you frees me to trust you again in deeper and in new ways. Trust can flourish only if it flows both ways.

7. *Trust is linked to dependability and predictability.* Over and over again, it has been shown that we will trust another person more easily and more deeply if we believe we can depend on them. My trust will be more extensive if I can predict how you will respond — even in little things like being on time for a meal, phoning when you're out of town for one night, or putting your shoes where I won't stumble over them. Dependability is important. How crucial it is, then, when it comes to life-shaking things like accepting me when I've made a mistake, respecting my dignity in a major disagreement, providing me with freedom to be myself.

Predictability grows from dependability. If I can depend on you time after time, I learn that I can predict your behavior in many situations. And because I can depend on you and predict much of your behavior, I feel safe in trusting you.

8. *Trust thrives in a climate of openness and self-disclosure.* I can't trust very well if the other is closed, particularly if that person is deliberately hiding things from me. I become fearful because of the unknown; I trust less. If married partners are to create a bond of trust between them, they must be appropriately open with each other and practice self-disclosure.

The word "appropriate" is critical. We aren't talking about absolute openness at any time either partner feels like saying anything whatsoever. The openness which builds trust is sensitive to the needs of the other. Timing must be considered. If I am open with you, are you ready to receive what I disclose?

Both partners must work at being open. It can't be a one-way street. What the partner discloses must be received with understanding. This doesn't necessarily indicate agreement. The process of self-disclosure and listening, which we discussed in an earlier theme, is central to trust formation.

9. *A caring and loving environment promotes trust.* I can trust another person if I'm convinced that the other cares for me deeply and loves me completely. Knowing that I am loved helps me believe that the risks of trust are worthwhile. The opportunity to be loved and to give love propels me toward building a trusting bond with another. If I begin to doubt my mate's love for me or to feel my partner doesn't care anymore, I grow less trusting.

10. *Trust is more likely to happen if we expect each other to be trustworthy.* Many researchers have observed that assumptions and expectations influence very much who we become in any given relationship. We tend to conform to what it is we believe the other person expects of us. If we both expect each other to be trustworthy, there is a good chance we will be. On the contrary, if we continually worry about and question the behavior of our spouse, we create an environment of untrustworthiness.

11. *While trust is slow and often difficult to develop, it can be destroyed quickly and easily.* One act, completed within a short time, can erase trust which has taken months and even years to build. While I learn to trust in the context of your acceptance and love, I become defensive and fearful when you behave in an untrustworthy way. Feeling betrayed, I immediately protect myself from the pain and hurt. Trust is like a vapor. It's there, strong and evident. But an unexpected change in atmosphere can blow it away.

12. *There are ways to build trust and ways to rebuild it when weakened.* There are things spouses can do to build and nurture trust. Taking risks, being open with thoughts and feelings, listening with understanding and acceptance, being dependable, expressing care and love —all contribute to building trust.

It's more difficult to rebuild trust when it has been broken: I trusted once; I took the risk, I was hurt, I can't and won't trust again. These thoughts are typical of a person who feels betrayed in a trusting relationship. Somehow, that person has to be given time, space, support, and love to recover lost trust. It demands a leap that can seem impossible for a long time. Initial trust building is slow. Rebuilding broken trust is ever so much slower. Sometimes, in the wake of deep hurt and pain, it never happens. The person ends up feeling isolated and cut off from spouse, self, and God.

These twelve characteristics demonstrate how complex it is to build and to maintain trust in a marital relationship. They also indicate that trust can be easily broken. The small word "trust" involves many relational dynamics.

Trust Building

While building trust is very complex, it is essential to the health and well-being of enduring marriages. It is integral to marital success and satisfaction. Trust must be nurtured and maintained if married persons are to become independent, free, yet deeply committed and bonded persons.

But what do we do to make this sustained trust happen? One insight we need to understand clearly is that trust building takes work, demanding considerable time and energy.

We must become trusting persons for each other, constantly taking the risk. Of course, we can be deeply hurt and there is the potential for much pain. But without risking the hurt and pain which might come, we can't experience the joy and fulfillment which does come with deepened oneness and bonding.

We must be trustworthy to build our mate's trust. We are called to take risks and to respond to the risks taken by the other. Mutuality calls us to take the risk of trusting, and to respond to the risk taken by the other by being trustworthy. We must be all that we can be as a person worthy of trust by our spouse. If trust is to deepen, we must each continue earning the right to be trusted.

Faith and Trust

Some important faith perspectives will add to our understanding at this point. While we are called to trust and be trustworthy, we do this within the limitations of our being human beings. We aren't perfect. We can't act always in completely trustworthy ways. Only God can be all that has been promised in a relationship. In our faith relationship with the Lord, we find One who is perfectly trustworthy. Our trust isn't in vain, nor is it ever betrayed.

Called to Trustworthiness

We are called to be trustworthy in our relationships just as God is trustworthy. As a married couple, our relationship is the arena where we test that the most. We intend and strive to be faithful in little things, like day-to-day tasks and communication, and in monumental things, like time, presence, sexuality, and closeness. But we discover we can't achieve the kind of unfailing, unchanging faithfulness God has for us. We fail. Our trustworthiness is fragile.

Human beings do make mistakes. We make less than perfect choices. We get caught between two goods but find that we can't choose both at once. We fail to be all that we would like to be. Personally, we (Jan and Myron) have struggled with time and presence. Our intentions are good. We plan quality time with each other. We intend to be present in times of need, of course, but beyond that, we plan periods together where we can enjoy being with each other. Our plans are right. We trust in them, and in each other. We intend to follow through. But, the actual time and presence may get cut considerably, or evaporate into virtually the bare essentials for long periods. Generally, we are busy being faithful to our jobs, our parenting, our friends, our church, our yard, and so on. For the sake of other important investments, we end up being less than we intend and want to be in our marriage.

Sometimes, too, spouses misunderstand behavior. I tell you I will do something. It's a promise, and I know you trust me. I do it. I believe I have done what I said I would do. In my eyes, I have been dependable. However, to you the picture isn't the same. Expectations weren't met. From your perspective, I wasn't as dependable as I "should" have been. Consequently, we begin to question each other's trustworthiness.

Forgiveness: The Remedy to Broken Trust

We've broken trust. What can we do? Our faith helps us. Deeply embedded in God's promises to us and Christ's action for us is forgiveness. God's generosity toward humanity in our failures and weaknesses is a model of how we need to treat each other. Forgiveness is a difficult process. It calls us to do some very hard things.

Sometimes we settle for an exchange of words: I'm sorry, please forgive me. I'll forgive you. But true forgiveness goes beyond words. It calls us to the renewal of a trusting relationship. What we have been to each other hasn't worked; we must create a new beginning and a new way of being who we need to be. We must say in our hearts, "I'll risk trusting you again." That can be terribly hard if the broken trust has led to deep pain and hurt. But if the relationship is to survive and be healthy, it has to happen. Living in an untrusting climate day after day breeds despair and nibbles at our faith in God. Such conditions eventually become intolerable.

It's difficult to initiate the process of forgiveness. It is a formidable challenge to say, "I'm sorry. I need a new beginning with you. I wasn't as trustworthy as I could or should have been."

Another challenge comes to the one who agrees to respond. "I do forgive you. I will walk with you into a new beginning. We can learn to trust and be trustworthy in new ways."

It's most likely that in the forgiveness process, both persons will discover where each could have done more to maintain the original trust. Both will find their own contribution to the broken trust in the relationship. When the forgiveness process has been worked completely through, the couple will likely be grateful that their relationship endured and is stronger because of it. Their trusting each other will now be more genuine and wiser in terms of expectations.

It's important to note that the healing of relational pain takes time. We don't transcend these hurts quickly. Many feelings about self and one's spouse have to be explored. Numerous thoughts and judgments have to be sorted through. To rush this process of exploration and sorting may lead to false truth where we each say to the other, "I trust you," but deep inside are filled with uncertainty and doubt.

Genuine forgiveness means letting go of the broken trust without intending to use it as a weapon in the relationship. Of course, the old saying "forgive and forget" isn't too realistic. Some of the events we remember most clearly and with great pain are those in which significant others failed to meet our expectations of trust. Even when we try our hardest to forget, the memories remain.

A healthier approach is trying to genuinely forgive the other person and resolving not to use memories of the events to punish, manipulate or bring further hurt to our mate. Occasionally, talking things through can be helpful. The forgiving process not only deepens the husband/wife relationship, but also makes possible a deeper faith relationship with a forgiving, trustworthy God.

Allow us (Myron and Jan) to reflect on our own experience: Our son was born when we were both in graduate school. I (Myron) was busy finishing a quarter's teaching and preparing to start a new one. Because of complications, Tim, our infant son, was transferred the first night to Children's Hospital several blocks away. Jan was hospitalized eight days. I came to the hospital as often as I could, given my other responsibilities. The days were long for Jan. She felt abandoned and alone. Tim's tiny, new life hung in a balance. Every day the pediatricians reported to her at the hospital: "We're doing all we can. We just have to wait." Jan relayed the reports to me. It was a dark and fearsome time.

It was months later that Jan told me that she had needed me more often than I'd been present. I reminded her that she had been very brave, and that she had said nothing about asking for my presence.

Through the years, we have looked at that event and learned much. I came to understand that underneath Jan's strong, brave appearance there had been a frightened, lonely person. Jan had to realize that the mounting medical costs, the home responsibilities, the teaching requirements, and the precarious life of our son created a mountain of worry for me. I did the best I could have, given the circumstances. However, if Jan had said clearly, "I need you," I would have been there.

Those circumstances weakened our relational trust for a time. But in engaging in the forgiving process, we discovered many things. We learned much about ourselves, our relationship, and what we wanted to be to each other in the future.

That is one of our trust issues. We have had many others and have learned from them. We continue to invest time and energy in building trust between us. We often ask for God's strength to keep us faithful and trustworthy, and to take the leap into the forgiveness process when we fall short.

EXPERIENCE

Instructions: Take time to reflect upon trust in your relationship as husband and wife. Then, respond to Items 1, 2, and 3. You may want to use very brief notes, but think about what you would like to share with each other. Try to learn from your thoughts. Move to Item 4 after you have shared and discussed Items 1 through 3.

Wife

1. Times when I have trusted you the most are:

2. An event I remember which weakened our trust is:

3. My rating of the way we have forgiven each other is:
   Poor   1   2   3   4   5   Excellent

Husband

1. Times when I have trusted you the most are:

2. An event I remember which weakened our trust is:

3. My rating of the way we have forgiven each other is:
   Poor   1   2   3   4   5   Excellent

Wife and Husband

4. A goal or two we would like to set to build and nurture trust in our relationship:

MEDITATION

*T*his I know: that God is on my side ... in God I put my trust, fearing nothing.

Ps 56:9, 11

*L*ord, hear our prayer:
We have trusted you but not as completely or faithfully as we ought.
Forgive us.
We have trusted each other, but not as completely or faithfully as we ought.
Forgive us.
We have sought to be trustworthy and have done better at some times than at others.
Forgive us.
Help us to mutually trust and forgive each other. Amen.

CHAPTER 8

NURTURING FAITH THROUGH MUTUAL NEED FULFILLMENT

REFLECTION

Dear Spouse,

Have I ever told you how much I need you? How can I? It's so hard to explain. I need you. I hope you know that. I need you like . . .

roses need rain
fish need the sea
babies need milk
cats need a scratching post
dogs need fire hydrants
elephants need space
actors need an audience
clowns need a face.

I need you; I want you to know how much. I DO NEED YOU!
With all my love,
Your Spouse

Marriage and Human Needs

"Marriage is a dynamic relationship between a man and a woman who are committed to the mutual satisfaction of their needs, the partner's as well as their own." This shorthand definition of marriage was given by Gregory Leville of Family Services of Philadelphia when he lectured in one of our doctoral seminary classes. He pointed out that this definition is not comprehensive. Marriage is more than mutual need fulfillment. But his point to the class was that without this key element, marriages collapse.

A marriage has its beginning in the needs of the two individuals. Every person has a unique need system which seeks fulfillment. Persons are aware of some of their needs; other needs tend to be subconscious, although they may be equally strong.

Human beings weren't created to be alone. We need other persons. We need God. Our initial attraction to other persons can usually be traced to a belief that somehow that other person or persons will meet some of our needs. If we discover that, indeed, our needs are being met, we pursue the relationship. We continue to invest time and energy. In contrast, if our needs seem to remain unfulfilled, we're likely to look for someone else who may bring us more rewards. Dating years are made up of this kind of sorting-out process. When "the one" is found and marriage is decided upon, an unwritten, often non-verbalized, agreement that the other will meet my needs is made.

In some cases, the primary need is to escape what is perceived as the oppressive influence of parents:

> *My father always ordered me around. I need a spouse who will let me be in control.*
> *My parents fought a lot. I need a spouse who will avoid fighting.*
> *My mother made all my decisions. I want to marry someone who will let me make up my own mind.*
> *My parents rarely showed overt love and affection. I want a spouse who will demonstrate love and caring unreservedly.*
> *My parents saved their money. I need a spending spouse.*

In other cases, the primary need is to preserve the perceived positive attributes found in parents.

> *My father always made me feel very secure. I need a spouse like him.*
> *My parents did many things together. I need a spouse who will do the same with me.*
> *My mother did everything for me. I need a servant spouse.*
> *My parents believed in having kids. I need a large family, too.*
> *My parents were active in church. I need a spouse who will be active with me in church affairs.*

The needs vary from person to person and couple to couple, but the underlying expectation is that this wonderful person is going to meet my needs perfectly forever. Of course, when the expectation is stated this bluntly, it appears naive and a bit ridiculous. It's an impossible load to lay on another person. It becomes even more complicated because the expectations are mutual. Not only, "I want my spouse to meet my needs," but also, "I'm expected to meet the needs of my spouse." How can this happen? Perhaps an exploration of some aspects of need fulfillment will broaden our understanding.

The Complexity of Human Need Systems

Need systems are complex. We pointed out earlier that many of our needs are subconscious. The needs of which we are aware may be only the tip of the iceberg. Persons may think they are marrying another because of some very healthy, positive reasons. In actuality, however, they may be marrying this individual because of more basic needs which are unknown and often not as healthy.

Needs operate at different levels. Abraham Maslow, the renowned psychologist, has done much to help us understand human needs and their order of importance. First, there are survival and safety needs—food, water, shelter—the very basic human needs. When these needs are met, we're hardly aware of them. But when we are satisfied that our basic needs will be met, then our growth needs—love, a sense of belonging, self-esteem, meaningfulness—begin to stand out in importance.

Many needs are shaped by life's experiences. A child who was abused by an uncontrolled parent will have needs different from one who was treated with love and respect. When two persons marry, they bring with them need systems which have developed out of their separate life histories. They may be similar. They may be quite different.

The complexity of needs interacts with all that happens in a marriage. Unconscious needs exert powerful influence on a person's life. One spouse explodes in anger, bringing amazement to both. Why and where did this outburst come from? It may be rooted in an unconscious need which had remained unfilled.

Levels of needs can help us see some other marriage dynamics more clearly. When there was enough money, all seemed well in a certain marriage. Unemployment caused the family budget to shrivel and the small savings to dwindle. Suddenly, a previously harmonious couple found themselves at odds in determining just what basic necessities are. One advocated selling the house; the other recoiled at the thought. Then, a new job brought added resources. The couple's lost harmony slowly returned as the previous standard of living was restored.

In another situation, foods and diet suddenly became a basic concern to a husband whose doctor informed him of his diabetic condition. He had been accustomed to eating and enjoying all of the many delicacies prepared by his wife. The diabetic condition brought to light a different need; simple foods carefully selected from the basic food groups and measured-out balanced meals at designated intervals. He was dealing with a basic survival issue to which he once gave little thought.

Needs based on life history emerge continually in a marriage. Spouses quickly learn where they stand together and where they differ as they build their life together. A pointed illustration of this was given us several years ago when we visited the home of some friends of ours prior to Christmas. Their tree was surrounded by an unbelievable number of packages brightly wrapped and decorated with yarns and bows. Our family reacted with shock. Their gift array made ours seem meager. They caught our amazed look and explained:

> She: I need lots of presents at Christmas. I can get along with almost nothing the rest of the year, but at Christmas I have to have presents for every one—even the dog. It's probably silly, but Christmas was a big thing in my family and I can't get over it.
> He: (smiling at her and us) She knows that I need to have Christmas paid for in cash. She saves all year. She also buys lots of cheap presents. I insist she stay within our budget. Some of these presents cost less than the paper.

We all laughed, but the point was well made.

Need Systems and Change

The needs one has at the time of marriage are far from permanent. They change with the natural progression of life and its crises.

Young adulthood is filled with needs related to human intimacy and closeness. It is a time of considerable drive to do one's best with the closest, dearest, and life-long friend, one's spouse. Joy flows from meeting the needs of one's mate. Great pleasure is found sexually, where one experiences profound depth in giving one's body to the other. Other relational needs are also given top priority.

As life moves on, personal needs surface with compelling force. A wife who once had her needs satisfied through closeness to her husband and in caring for children may begin to feel a need to fulfill personal goals of her own.

Recently on the *Good Morning, America* TV show a wife/mother was interviewed because of a "mothers' strike" she had conducted. As she explained her reasons for the strike she reflected, "I wanted my family to see that I have needs, too. I wanted them to treat me as a person. I need love and respect." She had asked other family members to assume more responsibility for household tasks, but personal affirmation was a far more urgent goal from her perspective. "I can do the chores," she said, "but I need their love. I need to know they care for me as a person, not a slave. I need to know that what I do for them is appreciated."

This mother went on strike. Others go back to school or to work. In one way or another, they demonstrate personal needs quite apart from spouse and family. Husbands/fathers have different, but similar personal needs, leading them to seek more leisure time, hobbies, job changes, and any number of other things that offer potential for fulfillment.

In later life, dramatic changes may occur in one's need system. Failing health, depleted energy, more unstructured time, and limited money all influence the needs of older adults.

In addition to these natural, emerging life changes, crises strike. Suddenly a host of new needs are presented. We discuss the impact of crises on marriage in a separate theme.

Changing Need Systems and Marriage

As persons grow and mature, needs change. Life crises, too, may radically redefine need systems. All of this is natural. What does it mean for marriage? Two implications stand out.

First, we must focus on the nature of the changes taking place in our lives. We can do much to reduce the frustration and depression caused by unmet needs if we can identify the new needs emerging within us. Old behaviors and routines which once gave great satisfaction may now grate and grind. We may not understand this if we are unaware of a changed need system operating in our lives.

Second, we must try to cultivate sensitivity to the changing needs of our spouse. We should expect a changing need system. Certainly, there is a comfortableness and security in knowing that the things we do meet the needs of our spouse. The problem is that what we do today may be satisfying but will be much less so five years from now. Being sensitive can help us understand the person our companion is becoming, can change our actions appropriately, and can help our spouse gain valuable insight into him- or herself through our attentive listening.

Communicating Needs

Needs must be communicated. In living with another as intimately and intensely as we do with a marriage partner, we often assume that the other knows our needs without being told. Without words, we say "My spouse knows me so well that my mind and feelings are transparent. I don't have to explain or report what I am thinking, feeling, or needing. My spouse already knows." Of course, such assumptions are open to great error. One's mind is not transparent; nor are one's deepest feelings always obvious. Adults become expert at wearing masks through which they appear to be thinking and feeling one thing, while in truth they are thinking and feeling something else.

It is true that because marriage partners live intimately, they often can assess the needs of their mate more accurately than anyone else. But it can't be assumed that they *always* know. It's our responsibility to tell the other, "Right now my needs are . . ." If we learn to tell the other of our needs, then the guesswork is unnecessary.

Even if the spouse accurately assesses the needs, there may be no clue as to what response is expected. We need to be clear about that level, too. "My needs are . . . and I think it might help if you would. . . ." Then both persons are assured that the needs have surfaced, and that some thought has been given as to what to do to meet those needs.

Counselors are familiar with a common marital complaint:

She: My husband knew what I needed and just ignored me. He didn't do anything.
He: Wait a minute! I knew something was wrong, but it was all so vague. The first thing I knew you were in a big pout, and I had no idea what I'd done wrong.
She: Well, if you didn't know, you should have!
He: Hold it! Who do you think I am, your own private mind reader? If that's what you want, forget it.

The conversation goes on. This couple has much to learn about communicating needs and listening sensitively to each other. This couple isn't unique; nor is their situation. Such an encounter is likely to happen every time one spouse assumes that the other knows, and that he or she will respond to needs without being told what those needs really are. You have probably experienced this; we have. In these situations, it's time to back up and begin again, making sure each is clear as to what needs are the issues and what can be done to meet them.

Mutuality and the Meeting of Needs

Need fulfillment in marriage requires mutuality. Perhaps more than any other kind of human relationship, the marital one thrives on the fulfillment of the needs of *both* persons. Each person enters the marriage expecting that the other will continue to meet needs throughout a lifetime of togetherness. Mutuality is essential. A situation in which one person consistently does the giving and the other the receiving will soon prove wearisome and unrewarding.

Mutuality involves a twosome committing themselves to the process of meeting each other's needs as effectively as possible through all of life's situations, routine as well as extraordinary.

Both must get involved. Both must learn to perceive as clearly as possible what the needs are. They must plan ways to meet those needs.

Mutual Expectations: Being Realistic

While mutuality is essential, some cautions are in order.

Sometimes mutual expectations aren't realistic. Sometimes a spouse will count on the other to meet every need: "All that I have hoped for and need will come true through my spouse." But no one person can meet all the needs of another throughout life. Other persons are important as well. We (Jan and Myron) have found friends and relatives to be crucial in supporting us as we attempt to meet each other's needs. We work at being all that we can be to each other. Beyond that, Jan has special friends; Myron has special friends; we have special friends together.

The way married companions perceive their needs may be unreasonable. They may expect the other to meet needs which they could possibly meet themselves. When this happens, the load becomes far too heavy.

An example from our work may make the point. We were leading a marriage enrichment event. A young wife complained that her life was miserable, with little reward. She worked all day at a laundromat. She would take her young son with her and try to amuse him. When she came home, she would cook dinner and straighten the house. Each day, she fell into bed exhausted. Her husband complained that sometimes she ignored his need for sex. When we inquired into his life, we discovered he carried a part-time job and was involved in a rigorous graduate school program. "I'm tired and hungry when I get home," he said. "I need to have dinner and relax."

It's likely both of them felt the need to have a meal prepared and the clean-up work done. Culturally, she felt the pressure to do it: "I feel so guilty if I don't," she confessed. This couple's experience shared at our meeting provoked lively discussion. The group talked about various situations in which spouses feel the other should be meeting a particular need, when in fact a more reasonable solution should be sought.

Mutuality isn't a rigid *quid pro quo* (this for that). Some couples behave in this way when they attack the frustrations of meeting mutual needs by bargaining: "I will do *this* for you, if you'll do *that* for me." While this approach can at times be useful, it isn't satisfactory when used extensively or exclusively.

Balance is required. Over a marriage's history, there must be a balance between giving and receiving. Of course, there are periods when one person's needs so outweigh the other's that the giving/receiving tends to be one way. These are to be expected and can be balanced out in the long haul.

Mutual Need Fulfillment: A Faith Perspective

How does mutual need fulfillment interact with our growing faith? When we talk about needs, we are immediately confronted by our humanness. We need God. We need other persons. We need so many things. But we delude ourselves into believing we need much more than we actually do. We take more than our share of resources, believing that some day all of our needs will be met and we will be happy. We convince ourselves that we need to work more and feel guilty or lazy if we don't. There are many other ways by which we are confronted with the limitations of our humanity.

Pride and Self-Sufficiency

In dealing with each other's needs, we come up against our pride and self-sufficiency. For some, it's terribly embarrassing and almost sinful to say, "I need something from you." Underlying this viewpoint is the attitude, "I can do all that is necessary. I am self-sufficient." American rugged individualism has reinforced this attitude. We regard ourselves as failures if we can't be self-contained. This attitude separates us from God, from other persons, and quite often from our spouses.

Pride afflicts marriage partners who believe they can and should be everything that the other needs. When they can't meet that standard, they experience feelings of failure and guilt. The verdict meted out to the self is: "Somehow I ought to be more than I am."

Only God can wholly meet our needs for acceptance, forgiveness, love, and purpose. We can't be all things to other persons—even a beloved spouse. If we could, we would be more than mortal human beings.

Giving and Receiving

Mutual need fulfillment in marriage offers an unequaled opportunity to engage in the virtues of giving and receiving esteemed by our faith. Because the dynamics of giving/receiving are imperfect, couples are challenged by situations calling for patience and forgiveness.

> *In meeting the needs of my spouse I give*
> *day after day, year after year*
> *on his or her terms as well as my own*
> *at greater depth than may be comfortable*
> *in moments when I feel like receiving*
> *rather than giving*
> *from the inner resources of my*
> *being.*

Giving is easier at some times than at others. Some persons always find it hard. It involves too much risk. The other person may not understand the gift or even accept it. The gift may not adequately meet the need of the other, even though it's the best one can do. There is risk in giving yourself, but in doing so you deepen your understanding of God's great gift of self to us, our Lord Jesus Christ.

For other persons, receiving is more difficult than giving. To receive implies dependency—needing other persons. It indicates that one isn't sufficiently self-contained, nor whole, nor strong. For such persons, receiving shows weakness, and they cannot allow themselves to be vulnerable in this way. Interestingly, it's often persons generous in giving who are uncomfortable in receiving.

Jan's father was like that. He gave in quiet, beautiful ways to others but seemed to resent it when others tried to return the gift of self. The process of giving and receiving became complicated. It was only as Dad Duncan became old and weak that he came to terms with receiving. He was forced to accept help for survival. Finally the door was opened to repay all the gifts he had given to others over the years. Much relational healing took place during his last years.

* * * * *

In marriage, we need to balance our giving and receiving. This may present a difficult hurdle for some of us, but attempting to meet the challenge will help nurture our growth as faith partners.

EXERCISE

Instructions: Below are three items for each spouse to complete separately. When you have compared and discussed them, the fourth item should be completed together as an act of love and commitment.

Husband

1. When I think of how you have met my needs in the past, these two things stand out:

    a.

    b.

2. These three things stand out as I think of the many needs you meet in my life right now:

    a.

    b.

    c.

3. Some need areas (yours or mine) I'd like to talk more about include:

    a.

    b.

    c.

Wife

1. When I think of how you have met my needs in the past, these two things stand out:

    a.

    b.

2. These three things stand out as I think of the many needs you meet in my life right now:

    a.

    b.

    c.

3. Some need areas (yours or mine) I'd like to talk more about include:

    a.

    b.

    c.

Husband and Wife

4. Express in your own way gratitude and appreciation to each other for your life together. Commit yourselves to the continued meeting of each other's needs.

MEDITATION

*As the hart longs for flowing streams,
so longs my soul for thee, O God.
My soul thirsts for God.*

Ps 42:1-2

I need you, O God. I love you;
I want to serve you.
Help my unbelief.

I need my spouse.
My spouse needs me.
Guide us in our life as
we continue to learn
to give and receive.

Thank you
for being
present in our
relationship
and
in all of life.
Amen.

CHAPTER 9

NURTURING FAITH THROUGH LIFE'S CHANGES

REFLECTION

Life
Joy, Pain
Gift of Love
Like a River
Flowing into the Unknown
Change

For centuries, poets, songwriters, and authors have described life as a flowing river. Somewhere there is a beginning, a source. From that point on, the flow cannot be stopped. The character of the river changes, growing from a gurgling stream to a surging river, and the water flows on until it is lost in the sea.

Persons Change

Life is like that river. It begins and then pushes on relentlessly through time until it ends in death and the new life beyond. As birthdays pass, persons change. Each of us is somewhat different today from yesterday, this year from last, this decade from ten years ago.

Children, especially, change rapidly. It's difficult to believe that last year's babbling baby is this year's chattering toddler. The toddler becomes a preschooler; then come kindergarten and grade school.

Then come the rough years. The eighteen-inch, seven pound, nine ounce, helpless infant grows to be a six-foot-two, one-hundred-eighty-three pound hulk in a twenty-year span. He stands on the threshold of adulthood with its accompanying responsibilities and challenges. His brothers and sisters from the larger human family who entered life the same year, and who have continued to thrive, stand alongside him, each one with a unique set of vital statistics. The persons who have nurtured them and watched their progress muse: "My, how amazing. It seems like only yesterday . . ." Although expected, the changes have come so rapidly; they are hard to absorb. Life is like that.

The adult years are different, yet somehow very much the same. The changes from year to year may be subtle and less obvious. Yet, they are profound. Often, they happen without the person being aware of them. But recognized or not, continual change is an inevitable aspect of life. There is no escape. Life is like that.

Marital Bliss — Forever

One myth which couples frequently bring to their wedding is that life together will always be filled with exhilarating bliss. We'll be the same tomorrow as we are today . . . very much for each other, physically the same, totally in love, and expecting the best. Although we know that our parents struggled with their problems, that other couples have met one hurdle after another, somehow, we expect things to be different for us. Our love, we think, is so real, so vital, and so intense that we'll be sustained through it all.

This myth lasts longer for some couples than for others. Sometimes, it explodes that very wedding night when an unrewarding, unfulfilling sexual encounter is experienced. It can take days, weeks, or months, but eventually it happens. One person realizes that "My spouse is someone other than the person I thought I married. Some things have continued as before, but others have disappeared. Strange, new dimensions I didn't know about have emerged. In some ways, this person is the same. In others, vastly different." The other spouse is quietly thinking similar thoughts. They each realize, that to some degree, they have married a stranger.

Marriages Change

Believing that "once married always married in the same way to the same person," is naive. It is more realistic to recognize that long-term marriages are filled with change. As the persons change, so does the marriage. When the marital relationship is redefined in any way, the persons involved in the relationship feel the impact. Some scholars and therapists point to the need to renew marriage covenants at critical points. As my spouse becomes a new and different person, I am faced with the challenge to renew my covenant, to live in new ways which fit the new person my spouse has become. The same challenge faces my spouse when changes in me are noted. Such renewal calls for time and energy. Maintaining a marriage which is meaningful and vital through a lifetime requires ongoing attention. Although many couples assume that good marriages just happen, a number of voices are being raised to stress what some people have long suspected: good, rewarding marriages require hard work.

Where does all the change come from? Wouldn't it be simpler if there were no change? Why do we have to change? What if we're happy and comfortable the way we are? Can't we do something to stay that way?

To focus on life and its changing character inevitably raises questions. Many of them are never answered to our satisfaction because we really want definitive answers. We want the assurance that we can "lock in" to some of the best moments of our lives and stay that way. Life is not like that. This is hard to accept at times. Change is difficult to cope with.

Two Sources of Change

Two ways of viewing change may provide us with some insight. Some change arises primarily from within persons as they progress through their life's pilgrimage. Other change is external in terms of its source.

Internal Changes

Psychologists have pointed out that we face certain, rather predictable tasks as we go through life. We learn to sit, walk, talk, throw balls, and play soccer on a progressive schedule. Teachers shape their lessons with the developmental tasks of children in mind because they know these internal challenges correspond to teachable moments in the lives of their learners.

Adults, too, have their tasks, passages, or crises to undergo. Young persons in their twenties try to enter more fully into the adult world. They make decisions about education, jobs, marriage, life-style, possessions, and a myriad of other significant and not so significant things. They learn in a new way what responsibility is all about. Some of their decisions are better and more productive than others.

Those in their thirties try to make good at whatever they are doing. They want to avoid failure. They seek success and achievement. At the same time, they may feel bored and boxed in. They begin to ask: "Is life going to be like this forever?" Sometimes they'll launch out in totally new directions.

The forties can be, and frequently are, a time of turbulence. Life takes on a new urgency. Suddenly old age doesn't seem very far away. Dreams may remain unfulfilled. The lasting happiness so long desired has never materialized. Persons in their forties ask: "Who am I? What do I want to be? What will I do with the rest of my life?"

By the time the fifties arrive, people often discover that what really counts isn't achievement and success, but family and friends. As one's own physical limitations and those of others become evident, the realization that life is tenuous becomes clear. Each day becomes precious.

In the sixties and seventies, the reality of aging becomes starkly present. Death has to be faced with a new realism. Limitations of many kinds increase. It's another period of redefinition. Persons are compelled to look back and face life as it has been, with all of its successes and failures. This is a time to accept and realize that the tapestry of who we are today has been woven from the threads of our past life. Remembering is important at this age.

This is all, of course, quite general. Books have been written on the details of each stage. Any stage can take a number of forms. Inevitably, we experience life's stages through the decades of our span of life. And in doing so, we continually weave our own life tapestries. The texture of one person's stages may bear little resemblance to another's.

Some scholars maintain that there is a rhythm to these life changes. A period of active searching and disconcerting upheaval is likely to be followed by a time of stability and relative calm. Such certainty lasts only until the next period of seeking begins.

The two individuals who have been joined together in marriage are not preserved from personal change associated with the passing of time. Rather, changing persons are to be expected in a long-term marriage. A wife in her twenties felt rewarded and fulfilled by supporting her husband's dream and goals. But in her thirties her own needs and dreams deserve her energies and his active support. If her spouse is unaware or insensitive to this internal shift, he may perceive her as contradictory, disloyal, and totally unreasonable. Another couple, feeling secure with a steady income during their late thirties and early forties, may be challenged by the husband's decision that he simply can't continue doing the same thing day in and day out for the rest of his life. He is willing to risk the family's security for what he sees as a greater opportunity for happiness. His wife may recoil from the prospect of beginning again at this life juncture.

Internal changes come in many ways and result in a variety of new behaviors and decisions. Perhaps the shock of these can be cushioned if we realize that change in life is inevitable. The key is to expect the changes and to try to understand and respond to them.

External Factors

External factors—children growing older, aged parents becoming dependent, natural calamities (earthquakes, tornadoes, hurricanes, floods), fluctuating economic conditions, death of significant others—create conditions to which spouses must respond. These experiences cause changes in the persons involved. A marriage feels the effect. Such external factors are a second major source of change. Examples might clarify how external factors can impinge on a marriage.

Dick and Marge were in their late forties when Dick's mother became very ill. He began to spend his weekends driving one-hundred-fifty miles to be with his parents. He invested many hours in helping sort out their medical bills. He began channeling some of his and Marge's own money into meeting the mounting expenses. Marge was shocked. Dick had never seemed particularly close to either of his parents. In fact, he had often been overtly critical of them. Suddenly, he had become the devoted, loyal son. It was too much for Marge to comprehend.

Another example comes from Jan's experience. In 1964, a major flood ravaged parts of Denver, Colorado. Her parents lived on a farm some miles outside the city. The flood waters damaged many of the buildings, making them unusable. Amazingly, the house escaped extensive damage, except for the two cellars which filled with grimy, muddy water. Both Dad and Mom Duncan were in their seventies. Their discouragement was deep. They didn't know how to draw resources together to begin again. Earlier in their lives, trials and calamities had inspired them to think creatively and they had pooled their energies to push on and make new beginnings. Now, despair and gloom pervaded their lives and their relationship. It was a dark and threatening time. They both had changed. Their relationship had changed. Life had changed.

External changes often hit as suddenly as a lightning bolt on a humid summer afternoon. Yesterday, everything seemed so normal and predictable. Then with a ring of the telephone, new things become top priority. The marriage partners must respond to the situation, their own internal state, and the effects on their relationship.

The Interrelatedness of Internal and External Change

Although internal and external change can be separated when writing a book, it is not always separate in real life. Just when I feel the need to find new directions and answers for my life, some external crisis may complicate the process. I feel overwhelmed. Life is like that.

Decision Making and Marital Change

In addition to internal developmental growth and external factors, many changes in the lives of married partners relate to decisions made by either spouse or jointly by the two of them. Decisions are made, and the marriage absorbs the accompanying changes almost without notice. Other changes are quite the opposite. The amount and magnitude is crushing and totally unmanageable.

Career and job decisions involve new considerations for a marital relationship. At one time, it was rare to find a married woman who considered her job to be of equal importance to that of her spouse. That is not true today. The number of dual-career couples is rising. Sometimes, both persons work because of choice and the quest for fulfillment. In other cases, maintaining a particular standard of living and economic survival are the reason. In either case, difficult choices must be made. Changes are inevitable.

Drastic changes are often felt in the family where the woman who has remained in the home as wife and mother becomes a member of the workforce outside the home. Household tasks suddenly belong to every family member or they don't get done.

Career changes happen more routinely. People go back to school to retool for something new. Sometimes, they start to move in a new direction. As the persons change, the marriage changes as well.

Decisions about family life affect one's life. The most dramatic decision is to marry in the first place. If two individuals are to live together and get anything done, they must adjust to each other's ways. They discover that some changes take longer than others.

Becoming parents brings more changes than many persons realize. The first baby and the changes it brings about can be shocking. It begins with pregnancy itself. The wife struggles with morning sickness, a changing body image, and fluctuations in energy. She becomes absorbed in the creative miracle occurring within her body. Her moods may be unpredictable. The husband begins to sense that even before birth, the attention his wife gives him is now shared with the baby. After the birth, the changes are too numerous to list: hundreds of diapers to change, clothes to be washed, meals to be prepared, baths to be given, and rocker miles to be chalked off as a restless baby is calmed. Mother is a changed person; father is a changed person. Their relationship has changed. Life is like that.

It's naive to think that a second baby brings considerably less change than the first. Parents discover that the parenting time they had devoted to one child now has to be divided between two. And rarely are two children the same. The first was calm, happy, and never had croup. The second is active, fussy, and croupy much of the time. The third child is different again.

While children entering a home bring change, so do children leaving the home. A friend recently wrote us a letter about what to expect as our daughter, Melody, leaves home for the first time to enter college. We were told that we will miss her at unexpected moments. The dishes and the wash will grow smaller. The house will be quieter. The messes left on the dining room table will be less frequent. It dawned on us then, that there simply is no stable period in parenting. We change when they are born. We change as they grow up. We change again as they leave. Life is like that.

Children aren't the only family members who bring change to a marriage. Aged parents may become too feeble to care for themselves independently. Their need for help and supervision grows. Senior citizen clusters or nursing homes may be too expensive or foreboding. It is decided that they'll come to live with the family, at least temporarily. All kinds of changes occur at this point — some good, some not so good, but nearly all very difficult. Life is like that.

Geographic moves bring change. Couples will move for all kinds of reasons: it may be demanded by a job, or it may be a free decision to move away from something, or perhaps to something. Whatever the reason, moves bring change. Studies indicate that moving to new locations is one of the most stressful things human beings undertake. Rarely do we estimate accurately the amount of energy we have to invest to make a smooth adjustment. CHANGE seems to scream out from everywhere. Life in a new place is like that.

Retirement can be a formidable period of change, particularly if one's job was crucial in defining one's identity. Where once there was the pressure of having too much to do, there is now a vacuum. Whereas, before spouses couldn't find enough time to be together, now they find virtually no separateness. New, pressing fears about money appear. Health agendas emerge. How different from the wedding day when we had the illusion that we would always be the same. Life is like that.

One of the most overwhelming periods of change is when death claims one spouse and leaves the other to face life alone. Only memories continue the relationship. Sadly, life and death are like that.

Change is all around. Sometimes it brings goodness and happiness into our lives. At other times, it brings sadness. Always, it demands energy to cope. Couples discover that a strong, abiding faith in the presence and power of God can sustain them, offer them vision, and challenge them to move on.

But they'll discover that even their faith has changed. As life experiences accumulate, they begin to think about God in new ways. They feel differently about their relationship with God and its importance to them. Their faith emotions change. They find that their ways of living out their Christian commitment are different. As life's seasons come and go, their ways of relating with God are affected. Some persons trust in and rely more deeply on God as they deal with life experiences. Others move away until they find it difficult to know whether they believe and trust in God or not. Many people fluctuate in their faith relationship, experiencing a close faith walk for a period, but drifting away at other times. Their faith tapestry becomes a patchwork of closeness and distance to the Eternal One.

People change. But biblical promise, tradition, and our experiences assure us that God is trustworthy. God is present and involved in life, accepting and loving us. In this *being-for-us,* God doesn't change.

Expanding Faith Commitment

As life passes, people respond more fully as responsible faith persons. Researchers are just beginning to gain insight into this developmental process of faith. One thing which stands out is that our faith grows and changes just as we do. The faith relationship which undergirds the initial marriage covenant lacks the depth and maturity found in a faith relationship which is nurtured through the years.

* * * * *

Changes are inevitable throughout one's life. Life is like that. Faith changes are also inevitable. Faith is like that, too. How those changes affect us and what we do with them depend on the decisions we make and the attitudes we cultivate. We can choose to wallow in bitterness or to work through the pain and hurt, thereby freeing ourselves to move on. There are thousands of choices to be made. We can choose to nurture our faith relationship, enabling it to expand, to deepen, and to grow. Or, we can choose to live as if our relationship with God were of little or no value. This latter choice leaves our faith capacities untested and unfulfilled.

We have no choice about change: in ourselves, in others, in all of life. We do have choices about the shape change will take and our response to it. Positive decisions can nurture our life with God.

Change
Always Present
Coming as Surprises
Chosen by Us
Pushing Us into Newness
Life

EXERCISE

Instructions: Below are a number of items to discuss with your spouse. Select those that fit your relationship and your situation. Share your thoughts and feelings. You may want to have several sharing periods. This is a list to which you may want to return later in your marriage. Some items will apply more then than they do today.

List of Items To Discuss

1. Some of the differences in you that I became aware of early in our marriage:

2. Some of the most significant changes that have happened in my life during our marriage:

3. External factors I believe have caused us to change and how we coped with them:

4. Job and career decisions which have caused us to change:

5. Decisions regarding children and the resulting changes:

6. Geographic moves and the adjustments necessary:

7. Changes related to our older years and how we are coping:

8. My awareness of how God has been present in the midst of change —yours, mine, ours:

MEDITATION

We're growing older together, Lord,
   My spouse and I.
We've had our good times and our bad times in the past.
There will be more of each, I know that.
Through it all I've changed, Lord,
   the same in some ways different in others.
My spouse has changed, too,
   different in many ways the same in others.
Our relationship has changed.
   That's good; it has to change or we wouldn't be together.
Thank you, Lord, for being with us in it all.
            You are the same yesterday,
               today, and forever.
            Our trust is in you. Amen.

CHAPTER 10

NURTURING FAITH THROUGH CRISES

REFLECTION

A Life-Changing Crisis

They were mountain people. They were hikers. They were backpackers. They were campers. They loved God's creation and spent much time enjoying it and caring for it.

They were middle-aged people. Much of life was behind them—the kids were all raised and gone from home, except when they returned for summer and Christmas vacations. Much of life lay ahead of them also. His job, her job, and new freedom from the responsibilities of parenting offered exciting new opportunities. Many possibilities lay on the horizon. Plans and dreams that had been postponed for years were within reach. They loved each other. They loved and served God.

Then it happened. They decided to drive late. It would give them more time when they got there. He was sleepy so she took the wheel. It's not totally clear what happened. Given the monotonous effect of the road in the darkness and the lateness of the hour, even the disc jockey's friendly rambling lost its power in keeping her alert. She sang until her voice wearied. It was just for a second that she drifted to sleep. That second was critical. The car jammed head-on into a concrete embankment, bounced off, and rolled over. From that second on, things were a blur. There was an eternity of waiting, the sound of faraway voices, then the sirens, the moving, the hospital lights, the smell of antiseptics, the pain, and the drugged sleep. Then there was the waking.

She opened her eyes and looked around. She tried to move, but the pain stopped her. A nurse gave her the short story. She had been in a horrible accident, suffering a concussion, with multiple wounds and abrasions requiring numerous stitches on various parts of her body. The two casts on her legs were to facilitate proper healing of the broken bones. The doctor would be available soon to explain the details and answer questions. In the meantime, she should rest.

"Wait," she called as the nurse turned to leave. She asked about *him*. The nurse hesitated. "He's not dead?" she asked with an anxiety that betrayed a critical question. "No," the nurse responded, shaking her head. "They flew him to University Hospital. He needed the specialists and the equipment. The doctor will be here soon." The nurse finished her sentence, checked the IV, and left.

"What about him?" she asked the doctor. He smiled and said, "Let's talk about you first." He explained the nature of her injuries. There was too much to absorb. The legs were the worst. It would take months. She heard that. There would be therapy. She heard that, too. There could be more surgery. "More?"

"Yes, we did all we could when you came."

She stared at the doctor. "What about him?"

"Well, he's seriously injured. There's a spinal injury, but we can't tell how much or how severe. He's in good hands at University Hospital. They'll take good care of him."

"What does it mean?"

"We really don't know yet. The first step was to get him to the best doctors and the best equipment. It will take some time."

"How much?"

"I don't know. A week or so for testing, probably."

"Oh, God," she murmured, partly as an exclamation and partly as a prayer. Tears flooded her eyes and raced down her face, splashing onto the hospital gown. She felt sick, alone, and empty. It hurt to move. Her mind was muddled; her emotions jumbled. She didn't notice the doctor leave the room.

Their crisis. This was the beginning. The beginning marked a permanent life change. Their bodies were never to be the same again. Her legs and ankles healed slowly. It was decided more surgery was necessary. Months of physical therapy brought slow, slow progress toward walking again.

His injury was a severely damaged spinal cord. His arms moved, but from the waist down he had only marginal control and movement — virtually no bowel and no bladder control. His basic therapy was to learn how to live with the condition. The final answer wasn't in. Any potential healing would be very, very slow — years rather than months — in being realized.

She faced her own body condition with courage. Emotionally, though, she was a wreck. The guilt of what happened to him engulfed her. She floundered under its weight. It blocked her from being able to see any future. She tried to bury herself in the past. It was futile. His broken body was a constant reminder. They faced an uncertain future.

Such a crisis is a permanent one. It changes one's life in a dramatic way. This is one story; but there are others — a first-born child with Down's Syndrome, a paralyzing stroke, loss of a financial fortune, a tragic divorce, and so on.

A Long-Range Crisis

It was almost ten years ago when a crisis hit us. Jan collapsed while on a business trip. It took months for doctors to diagnose the problem. They discovered she had EB virus which had invaded her central nervous system. One specialist predicted that it could take a decade before we would know the extent of permanent injury to her nervous system and the possibility of healing. As months became years, she continued to improve and gain health. Only those who know her well are aware of the energy she invests to maintain a strong, vigorous body. As years have passed, her own life and our lives together have become virtually normal. We think of her past illness but we have moved on to other of life's agenda. We have new challenges and new crises to face.

This crisis involving Jan was long-range in nature. It didn't pass quickly. When the doctors said it could be a number of months, we thought we couldn't face it. Then it stretched into years, and we managed it day by day. Finally, there came a time when we were able to close the door and say, "It is finished. Let's move on."

A Short-Range Crisis

When the steel mill cutbacks came, Ray knew his job was in jeopardy. He had survived the first couple of layoffs, but he knew if there were more, his time would come. It did. The official notice came as no surprise. Local news media had been predicting another cutback for at least two weeks. There would be some income for the weeks ahead, but there was no job and that hurt. In one sense, they were lucky because Chris had her job at the supermarket. They could and would survive it.

It was nearly a year before Ray had anything more than a day's work here or there. He was able finally to join the maintenance staff at a college fifteen miles away. It wasn't ideal. The pay was less and the distance was farther. But it was a job and the immediate crisis was remedied.

This crisis was short-range. It lasted for a significant period of time, but then it passed. The couple were able to reinvest their energies.

A Temporary Crisis

Marge met a crisis of sorts when her car skidded out of control on an icy road. The repair work was extensive, and the bill was high. Fortunately, Marge was not hurt. The biggest hurdle was to pay the "deductible" bill and to provide transportation for the family until the car was repaired. Ron, her husband, was obviously irritated. They were both frustrated and angry. They didn't need all of this. Their regular bills were high enough. But now, there was a new one, not to mention the added inconvenience. At the time, it seemed like an insurmountable crisis. One week later, with the car repaired and payments arranged, Marge and Ron hardly remembered last week and its crisis.

This crisis Marge and Ron faced was immediate and, for the most part, temporary. While the budget had to be stretched out for several months, life was back to normal in a week.

A Crisis Is a Crisis Is a Crisis

To most of us, any crisis is genuine and severe. At the time, we don't think about the permanency or gravity of what is happening. We simply know that some set of circumstances has disrupted our lives. The way we usually live doesn't work any more. We feel pushed to do everything we can to escape the tension and return to normal.

Furthermore, there is no *good* time for a crisis. It simply comes and we have to respond as effectively as we can. Rarely can we exert much control over it. A crisis strikes like a lightning bolt. At one moment, life is so normal; at the next, it has all changed.

Human Response to Crises

Persons respond to crises differently. Some people make quick decisions. Others become paralyzed. Many of us handle certain kinds of crises as if we were pros at it, but we are devastated by others. Crises generate a host of feelings: panic, anger, defeat, helplessness, and bewilderment. It's often difficult to harmonize our feelings with constructive action when a crisis strikes.

Every marriage faces the prospect of unexpected crises—somewhere, sometime. It's difficult to prepare for them because we usually have few clues as to what they will be, or when they will strike. If we act as if the next moment will surely bring a crisis, we'll miss much of life's routine joys. So most of us choose to live with the expectation that tomorrow will be much like today. That assumption works until a crisis strikes. Then we are stunned. Our first reaction is to feel that there is no way we will survive or handle this situation. Yet, amazingly, we do pull out of many adverse situations. We "muddle our way through." We surprise ourselves. When sufficient time has passed, it's common to hear a couple say, "I have no idea how we did it."

Emotional Coping

With crisis comes emotional pain. Responding at a personal level can be a drain. Then we may discover that our spouse is responding quite differently from ourselves. We wonder if he or she understands the crisis. One husband commented,: "Oh, my wife turns everything into a crisis." With that, the wife seemed hurt and angry that he failed to see her point of view. She lashed out by saying that without her intense reaction, nothing constructive would get done. There was truth in each viewpoint. The sad thing is that they both felt misunderstood and alone.

Even couples who respond similarly, or who understand and accept the reactions of the other, find themselves emotionally spent and exhausted during periods of crisis. They sense in the other a great need for support, but their own resources are low. Consequently, the relationship feels a strain.

If the crisis involves only one spouse in a dramatic way — such as illness, accident, or loss of a parent — there is still significant stress for the other. One mate has to face life in a whole new way. Self-identity is at stake: "I have to face the fact that life for me has changed. I am not and can not be the same." The other spouse watches the struggle, wishing to be more or do more than is possible: "If only it would have happened to me, I think I could handle that better. I feel so helpless." Both experience emotional trauma.

Physical Coping

Crises also can take their physical toll on a couple. Getting adequate rest becomes difficult. Worry may keep tired eyes open and weary minds active. Sleep doesn't come.

In some crises, the basic problem is finding time for sleeping. A family in our area cared for an aged grandmother as she moved toward death. For three months, she required constant care. Someone had to be with her at all times. As the days and weeks went by, it became more and more difficult to rest. "Some days we wondered if we could keep going. We thought we might die from exhaustion before Gramma died from cancer. It was a terrible time for us."

In our life together, we (Jan and Myron) have discovered that during periods of crisis, we find it hard to maintain our exercise schedule. Normally, we walk each day. Jan jumps on a trampoline and Myron lifts weights. During crises, the trampoline collects dust and the weights sit on the shelf. In the periods when we most need the exercise, we do not get it.

Coping with Time

Crises wreak havoc on our use of time. Routines are broken, schedules can't be met. It seems there isn't enough time. We try desperately to squeeze in extra minutes and hours which aren't there.

At other periods, time lies heavy. It drags along. Seconds seem like hours and hours stretch into an eternity. Whatever the situation, crises inevitably demand that we reorder the use of our time. Rarely is that an easy task. Often, it has to be done under great pressure and stress. We wish for better times.

Increasing the Potential for Handling Crises

Is it possible for spouses to increase their ability for handling crises? We believe it is. Not that the crises disappear, or that we breeze through them. Rather, by sharing the load the burden is made lighter, and the couple grows together rather than moving apart.

It's important to clarify and understand how each person is likely to respond in a crisis. We can then anticipate, to some extent, our similarities and our differences. We can accept each other for who we are. We can discover ways to be mutually helpful. If we don't have this insight, we may condemn and judge the other, thereby adding to the load rather than lightening it.

Spending Time Together

Spending time together is crucial. We need to talk, to express feelings, to vent bottled up frustration, and to voice inner anxiety. And if there is a need to talk, there is also a complementary need to listen. During a crisis, I may need to talk and have you listen. But I will have to remind myself that you, too, may need to talk and I will have to listen. And then again, there will be moments when we want simply to be together in silence—just being there for each other.

Jan's parents died almost one year apart, while we were in graduate school. Both had reached eighty and were not well. Yet their lives had been rich and full and we felt the simultaneous pain and relief together. But Jan had to face alone the loss and abandonment which come with the death of parents. There wasn't too much Myron could do, but his presence was important.

Voicing Mutual Needs

During the stress of a crisis, it's important to talk about needs in general and especially in relationship to each other. It's a time for saying directly, "I need from you. . . ." The pressure of the crisis may cause us to act in ways that are uncharacteristic during better times. We may withdraw, or lash out in anger, or exhibit any number of unexpected behaviors. Our life companion may have difficulty interpreting what is happening. It's appropriate to declare gently, "I need to have you tell me what is happening. I want to be more helpful, if I can." The importance of voicing our mutual needs was developed earlier in this book. We reinforce its importance here.

Sharing the Crisis

We can learn to deal with the crisis in mutually beneficial ways. Sometimes, rather predictable patterns emerge. For example, one spouse assumes the role of being strong and undauntable, becoming superhuman, controlling all emotions. Such a spouse can be a source of strength.

Yet, this show of strength may also prevent others from sharing the crisis fully. Such strength makes it difficult to share weakness. With a partner appearing so strong as to be unreachable, a person begins to feel as though there is nothing he or she can contribute. Underneath, however, strong people feel tension, hurt, anxiety, and pain in a crisis, too. They simply rely on showing strength as a way of saying to themselves and others: "I have this situation under control—as much as I possibly can."

During a crisis, I may need you to be strong for me. Your strength helps me believe in myself and in us. I don't feel quite as weak. But at the same time, you need to let me be strong for you. I want to help you believe in yourself, and in our potential to go on facing life together.

Sharing a crisis may mean being strong for each other. At other times, we may share our weakness and despair. These moments can seem heavy and fearsome, but they can also bind us together as strong human persons. When couples don't share a crisis fully, they may be torn apart by their isolation, rather than bound together by their relational strength.

Holding Each Other Accountable

In the midst of a crisis there is a heightened need to hold our spouse accountable. Our mate must do the same. We entered the marriage covenant to guard the well-being of each other's person and that of our marital relationship. Under stress, living out that responsibility can be forgotten. I will be inclined to invest my time and energy in every direction except in my companion whom I take for granted. I may even neglect my own health and emotional stability. Yet the one voice which has a chance of reaching me with its appeal to be more reasonable, and to take a look at alternatives, is that of my marriage partner, who is closest to me and knows me better at times than I know myself.

But it's difficult, even under the best of circumstances, to hold a spouse accountable. It's an even greater hurdle when tension and stress run high. Looking for the right timing, we put it off. Uncertain of the impact, we avoid it. We know it's a risky process, so we invent reasons why it's better not to do it. And while we delay, our mate continues to live in ways which tear into his or her personal well-being and our relational happiness.

* * * * *

Learning to spend time together, voicing our needs, sharing the depths of the experience, and holding each other accountable will be easier for us in periods of crisis if we have done these things during the ordinary course of life. The problem with beginning these during a crisis is that tension and stress are already high and expecting new behaviors during a crisis adds to the load. Being accustomed to these behaviors makes it easier to respond in spite of crisis overload.

Once a crisis has passed, reflection time is valuable to assess what happened and how we managed. We can use this hurdle to prepare for the next one—whenever it comes.

Crisis and Faith

How do crises intersect with our faith journey? It's an ancient insight on the part of humanity that a crisis can rekindle and revitalize a dwindling faith. In times of weakness, there is no question of our need for God. It is at these times that we desperately hope in God's faithfulness, despite the many ways we have been unfaithful to him. When faced with overwhelmingly negative experiences, we find ourselves forced to trust God more deeply than ever before.

As couples are led to deeper hope and trust, a counter stream of thoughts and questions may arise: Why did this happen? Why did it happen to *me?* To *us?* How can a loving God allow or maybe even cause this to happen? We have had our share of problems already. Why is there no justice? What is the meaning of all this?

Is this a contradiction?

In one perspective, we hope that God will be present with us. We trust that God will not forsake us, but will be beside us, around us, beneath us, behind us, before us, and within us so that we may endure. Crisis periods compel us to trust as we have never trusted before. What we have believed somewhat superficially we now affirm with great intensity.

Yet, from another perspective, our penetrating questions have no simple solutions. For centuries, people have asked the same questions and found no satisfactory answers. Still, we struggle for meaning and our questions ring out. God seems not to give answers to our questions.

The Presence of God

During the crises in our lives, we have leaned heavily on the promise that God will be present in the midst of it all, providing us with strength and resources sufficient for our needs. Sometimes God's presence has been felt very strongly. But there also have been periods when God has seemed far away, when there seemed no way to get in touch with him, when we felt alone and abandoned.

Interestingly, our awareness of God's presence has been rekindled most often through other persons. Sometimes we have done this for each other. On other occasions, it has been someone else who has spoken a word or been a presence to us. As we look back over our marriage, we do not doubt that God has been present to us. That assurance helps us as we face the future and the crises it may hold.

The Community of Faith

We have also discovered the absolute necessity of being supported by the community of faith. Earlier we indicated that our son had a long and severe illness during 1981 and 1982. A group of faithful friends let us know of their willingness to help in concrete ways. They sustained us. We made a list which was posted on the refrigerator door with names and phone numbers. We called and they answered. God was present to us through them.

Friends also ministered directly to Tim. They wrote, called, visited, helped build his button collection, and offered words of encouragement. Melody's friends supported her in many ways too. Through our friendships, we were all supported. God was there supporting us in and through our friends.

We have known persons embittered because they didn't receive as much support from the Christian community as they needed and expected. We believe that in most of those cases, the needs weren't voiced and/or made clear. The church can't be expected to read our minds. It's our responsibility to let it know we are facing a crisis and need the sustaining power of the Christian community. True, it may be hard for us to assume that responsibility. It may be so difficult that we don't act. But unless we do, we deprive ourselves of the life-sustaining power of a community of faith.

Crises and Faith Decisions

Crises are decisive moments in a marriage relationship. They can be turning points in our life journeys because they involve choice. Requiring courage and risk-taking, they offer opportunities to choose life with God. And if we choose such a trusting relationship with God, we are liberated from the chains of fear, paralysis, anxiety, panic, anger, defeat, bewilderment, and hasty but foolhardy decisions. The exercise of such faith in critical circumstances can draw us as married persons closer together. It can also draw us into a deeper relationship with a trustworthy God and the family of faith.

If we do not draw upon our faith in critical times, a deep chasm may develop in our relationship with God. The negative experiences of life may overwhelm and embitter us. We will be choosing death rather than life, evil rather than good. Crises call us to a deeper trust in God, to the God who is present even in the foxholes of life.

God is present in crisis. My faith, your faith, and our faith may be both deepened and tested as we walk through the valleys of life. We know that God is present to each of us and in our relationship.

EXERCISE

1. Identify and discuss some of the crises you have faced together.

2. Share your thinking in response to the following questions:
   How clear are we on how we respond to crisis?
   How faithful are we at spending time together during crisis periods?
   How able are we to express our crisis needs to each other and to the faith community?
   To what extent do we share the crisis in mutually helpful ways?
   To what extent do we hold each other accountable for personal and relational well-being?

3. Choose a specific crisis and assess how that crisis intersected with your faith by using the following scale. Share your reasons for marking the scales as you did.

   Husband
   (a) During the crisis, our trust in God was
   very weak   1   2   3   4   5   very strong

   (b) Our questions were
   few   1   2   3   4   5   many

   (c) As a result of the crisis, our faith
   wavered   1   2   3   4   5   deepened

   Wife
   (a) During the crisis, our trust in God was
   very weak   1   2   3   4   5   very strong

   (b) Our questions were
   few   1   2   3   4   5   many

   (c) As a result of the crisis, our faith
   wavered   1   2   3   4   5   deepened

MEDITATION

God is our shelter, our strength, ever ready to help in time of trouble, so we shall not be afraid when the earth gives way, when mountains tumble into the depths of the sea, and its waters roar and seethe, the mountains tottering as it heaves.

Psalm 46:1-3

Oh God, help us to trust you in the midst of life's crises. May we know that you are our shelter and our strength. Thank you for being with us. Amen.

CHAPTER 11

NURTURING FAITH THROUGH PARENTING

REFLECTION

SOME DAYS
ARE LIKE THIS:

"My kids are a real joy. I wear my parenting badge with pride."

OTHER DAYS
ARE LIKE THIS:

"My kids are a real pain. I think I'll turn in my parenting badge and forget the whole thing."

Of course, there aren't parenting badges to wear with pride, or to turn in with frustration. At least, we've not seen them.

Some days, parenting is fun, rewarding, and joy-producing. These days feel good. It seems worth it all. We exchange looks of pride and fulfillment.

But there are other days, for whatever reason, that don't go so well. If Melody and Tim, our two children, end the day feeling hurt and misunderstood, we feel frustrated, and view ourselves as failures. These are the occasions when we talk about turning in our parenting badges. Of course, we don't really do anything except resolve that tomorrow we'll be better parents.

The mention of turning in the parenting badge is a signal to each other that, for whatever reason, parenting hasn't gone well for us. We then open up the opportunity to talk about it, to vent feelings, and to receive support from each other.

Parenting — A Difficult Challenge

Many professionals who work and write in the area of marriage and the family attest that parenting is one of the most difficult relational tasks persons ever face. It involves eighteen or more years of care for each child, twenty-four-hour-a-day duty with no weekends or vacations. The responsibility of nurturing a helpless infant into an independent, wholesome adult is awesome. While one has considerable choice in selecting a spouse, there is virtually no choice in parenting.

It's quite possible to find oneself parenting a child whose personality and character are different from anything you would have custom ordered. There are no schools to train you thoroughly to parent. In fact, much of what you know about being a mom or a dad comes from the treatment you received from your mom and dad. Beyond your own experience as a child, you have to learn about parenting as you go.

This do-it-yourself approach has many pitfalls. Mistakes will be many. The process becomes even more complicated when you discover that something you learned worked well with your first child doesn't work at all with the second or third. It's all very awesome.

Some parents have said to us, "If we'd known all that we were getting into, we might not have done it." Others have confessed, "We simply wouldn't have had children if we knew what we know today. We weren't ready for it. It took more resources than we had available to us." These parents might very well at other times voice a more positive view. They may be merely stating their negative feelings in a safe climate. However, there is no question that parenting is a challenge which demands everything and more from us as individuals or as a couple.

Parenting — A Togetherness Task

Being parents requires commitment, patience, self-giving, persistence, and many other virtues, but most of all togetherness. If a father and mother aren't of one mind in being parents, on what it means, how to do it, and their goals, strain will develop in their relationship. Even when a couple seem to be of one mind on a theoretical level, they'll usually discover many points of disagreement when it comes to the doing.

These differences emerge early in parenthood. A young husband and wife may agree that the time is right for having a baby. When the pregnancy is confirmed, they both share the excitement. But as the woman becomes more and more involved with what is taking place in her body, the man may feel excluded. Once he had felt central in his wife's life, but now he is not so certain. When the baby actually arrives, the situation can worsen as the young mother finds herself tied to the needs of the infant.

Fathers, too, may experience the pressure of meeting the baby's needs. Husband and wife may have agreed to share the care of their newborn. But all too soon, the soiled diaper change late at night becomes a burden.

It may be difficult to parent together, but it's important. When parents aren't in agreement, children soon make that discovery. In an effort to exert power, have needs met, or gain affection, a child may pit one parent against the other. We have known couples who have been very much together in their parenting but who reported, "The kids discovered where we didn't agree and put the pressure on. How they did it, we don't know. They sensed it somehow." What parents haven't had such an experience?

There are two special circumstances occurring more frequently in our society. One is the *single parent situation* caused by divorce. (The situation is different when related to death because one parent is absolutely alone in the nurturing task.) When a marriage relationship becomes so fractured and painful that the couple choose to divorce, a central issue is who will do the parenting and how.

We believe that both parents are obligated and responsible. They may have chosen to sever the marriage relationship, but one can't choose to abandon being a parent. The challenge is formidable. Still, it's crucial that parents — in spite of hurt, pain, and alienation — negotiate ways to be together in the nurturing of their children. Many stories are told of children who pitted one parent against the other, adding to a bad situation. Togetherness in marriage is one thing. Togetherness in parenting is quite another. Divorced couples need to keep this distinction in mind as they work out parenting issues.

The second circumstance is what is called the *reconstituted* or *blended family*. Two persons decide to marry. One or both of them already have children. The situation demands the working out of complex relationship rules. Children are expected to accept parenting from a person who isn't their natural parent. The spouse is expected to act as parent, although not being the natural parent. This situation is not easy. Everyone involved faces complicated issues and tasks. It's especially critical that the couple be together in this case. They must not only know the strength of their own relationship, but they must also understand the bonding related to parenthood and the loyalties of children for their natural parents. It's in this mix of human emotion and relational ties that parenting must occur. Togetherness can be tremendously difficult, but it is essential.

Parenting — Some Faith Perspectives

We have found it helpful to keep certain truths about parenting in focus as we face the challenge of nurturing children into responsible adulthood. These insights give us purpose and sustain us when we feel discouraged.

(1) Children—Gifts of God

First, children are God's gift to us, whether naturally born or adopted. In her book *The Committed Marriage,* Elizabeth Achtemeier describes children in marriage as "Gifts of Extravagant Grace." An infant is a miracle of new life created by God. This new spark of life is entrusted to the care of an inexperienced man and woman who, over the years ahead, will nurture it, form it, love it, and eventually set it free to become what it is meant to be. Each child is unique and different. Each is a precious creation of human life demonstrating God's ongoing love and involvement with humanity. Most of us have had the experience of awe and wonderment as we gaze at the minute detail of the tiny fingers of a newborn—complete in every way, down to the fingernails. In such a tiny body, each breath points beyond itself to the Eternal. No two children are the same. Even parents of twins learn to identify one from the other. There's a poster which says "When God made me, the mold was thrown away." In a sense, every child is a custom-made gift.

Sometimes the daily demands of family living make parents feel as if children are more burdens than gifts. Marital satisfaction frequently goes down as parents try to complete all the tasks of family life. To say that children are gifts is to affirm that God has entrusted the next generation of humanity to our care. There is no guarantee that parenting will be easy or light. In reality, it's likely to be an ongoing challenge with many ups and downs. The gift entails responsibility.

(2) Parenting as Stewardship

If children are God's gifts, then as parents we are stewards of the treasured lives that have been given to us. Stewards are called to be faithful and as servants of the Master, our task is to do God's will; to be God's representatives in the nurturing task. In one sense, this responsibility seems weighty. Yet in another sense, it's freeing. Parents are God's representatives; they are not God. They are not perfect or unable to make an error. They are called to be faithful to God's purposes.

(3) God's Love—A Model for Parents

Parents are called to love their children. We are commanded to love others and so to show something of God's love. And the life arena where love begins and can be most difficult to express is within marriage and family relations. Too often we settle for superficial forms of love—sweet words which lack any element of tough love or justice.

God's love for us is a model of the kind of love we parents need to show our children.

God cares for humanity with a steadfast love. God cares about our well-being, our relationship with himself and others. God cares to the point of becoming involved in our history through Jesus Christ. As parents, then, our love must be a caring love that concerns itself with the well-being of our children. We must become deeply involved with them as they carve out their lives.

God's love for humanity is a giving love. God gives life and breath. God gives all that is. The greatest gift by far is God's gift of the Son, Jesus Christ, the gift of the divine Self.

Parents, in a different sense, give life to children. We provide a nurturing environment. God's example shows that we must give of ourselves. In our busy world, it's easy to give our children *things* that substitute for self—a picturesque home, tasty food, a good education. The difficult part is giving of ourselves—being fully available as a person, a friend, a parent. It's the gift of self which children will treasure for life.

God's love for us is a respecting love. It doesn't force us, manipulate us, or treat us as puppets. God's presence and love are powerful, yet leave us free. Our individuality is respected. We are given the freedom to choose life or death, light or darkness.

Parents often have considerable problem with this respecting love because it allows a child the freedom to be him- or herself, to say yes and no, and to hammer out a personal life. Since most children assert their individuality early, respecting it can be a frustrating challenge for parents.

While God's love is a love that leaves persons free, it's also a love which disciplines. These two dimensions stand in tension. God has made the requirements for full living very clear. When these requirements are ignored, there are consequences. God's message is this: "You are free to choose. If your choices cause you to ignore the requirements I have set for rightful living, then my love is tough."

As parents, we too must have a toughness in our love. Part of parenting involves establishing fair, reasonable, and appropriate standards and rules. When children choose to rebel and not meet the requirements, we must follow through with actions which lead our children to greater self-discipline. This kind of tough, strong love is not easy for us or our children. But without it, our love will be soft and won't help our children to evaluate and discipline themselves.

God's love is forgiving. Human beings don't always make the right choices. We fail and flounder. We overstep our bounds with God, others, and even ourselves. So, we find ourselves continually in need of forgiveness. God's forgiving love is there to meet our need.

Our love for our children should be like that. They will often stand in need of our forgiveness and we must be ready to give it. Many times *we* will need to ask to be forgiven. We aren't perfect as parents. We will make mistakes. Asking our children for forgiveness should be considered part of being a parent. Granting forgiveness and asking to be forgiven are both a central part of parenting love.

Being a loving parent is sometimes very hard. We hardly have energies to hold our own life together, let alone for loving those around us. As parents, we need to be mirrors to each other, to help us see how and what we are doing with our children. We need each other for support. When we feel like a failure or absolutely drained, our spouse can be the one who reaches out and says, "Come, let me help you. We're in this together." We must be a mini-team, whose task it is to become more loving of each other and the lives we are caring for.

(4) Nurturing Children in a Living Faith

We must love our children. We must also nurture their faith and train them in it. The Bible is very clear that parents are to teach their children the ways of God. From rising in the morning until retiring at night, we are to think consciously about training children in the faith (Dt 6:4-9).

Teaching children the faith is partially a matter of imparting information to them. It's good when children are introduced to bible characters and bible stories in the home. There are many fine books parents can use as resources. Each family has to find its own best way of doing it. Some parents read bible stories at night. We found that approach less productive than reading to them during summer vacation.

More importantly, we need to be aware that children are learning by watching us. They listen to our words, but far beyond that, they watch and observe as we act and feel. From us they learn what is "right." They learn how to act. They are exposed to our feelings. If we pray regularly, they learn that prayer is important. If we set a priority on ethical, loving behavior with others, they see and believe. Young children are imitators. They do what we do. The faith picture they see us painting in our lives has a powerful impact on what faith means to them. If we set many other things before our faith, investing great amounts of time and energy in them, children will learn that faith in

God is relatively unimportant compared to other things. If we make clear that our faith relationship guides and informs our life, our children will see faith as relevant and important.

Religious rituals can contribute meaningfully to a faith climate in the home. We've already mentioned prayer and bible reading. There are many other practices a family can develop. We put special emphasis on family devotions during Advent and Lent. We try to highlight Christmas and Easter as holy days. We add an overt faith dimension to birthdays. We have found our ways. Some of them come from Jan's family; some from Myron's; some, we have created ourselves. You can find your own. It has been good for us to think creatively and plan for the faith nurturing of our children.

(5) Parenting—A Call to Faithful Discipleship

Parenting is part of our calling as Christian disciples, as is prayer, Bible study, worship, service, and marriage. As disciples, we are responsible for being obedient and faithful, not perfect. We've known a number of parents who struggled intensely with the realization that they couldn't be perfect. We can only do the best we can to parent faithfully, given our resources. Our own family experiences have shaped us, strengthened us, and scarred us. We bring both our strengths and our scars with us as we parent. All that we have is not enough for us to achieve perfection, even though we would like very much to do so.

We know several young couples who carefully digested the best books on raising children prior to the birth of their first baby. They did well, practicing good principles with that growing baby. However, when the second child was born, they were confronted with the fact they couldn't be perfect parents given the demands of two young lives, or three or more.

Perfection is a goal we lay on ourselves. As Christians, we are called to be faithful and obedient to God's ways in our lives. This realization should free us to be ourselves and lighten our burden in marriage and in parenting.

(6) Parenting—An Invitation to Learning and Growth

Finally, parenting is an invitation to learning and growth in what it means to be a human being. It doesn't take long for parents to realize that the responsibilities and challenges of relating to children will continually push them to their limits. They will discover themselves to be finite creatures, rather than gods who can respond to every need and whim of their offspring.

There is no better way to learn humility, patience, understanding, and numerous other life lessons than by relating to one's children as they grow and weave their own life stories. The late Henry Fonda told of having great difficulty in saying to anyone, "I love you." In late adolescence his son, Peter, began to end every phone call with the phrase, "I love you, Dad." Henry reported that it took him some time, but eventually he began to respond in return, "I love you, too, Son." Before his death, he had grown to the point that he would be first to offer his statement of love. "I learned it from Peter," he said.

As children explore life and the world, they grow. Parents who walk alongside them grow, too. Parenting is a rare opportunity and challenge. Some days it's a joy; other days, a pain. Through all the days, faith will sustain the moms and dads who struggle to be all they can be to God, to each other, and to their children. Through this struggle of relational faithfulness, the faith of parents will be nurtured and deepened.

EXERCISE

Instructions: Below are four sets of questions. Discuss each one. When you have finished, take a moment to summarize what you've learned.

1. In what ways are we together in parenting? What goals do we need to set for growth in our togetherness?

2. How does our love for our children compare with the model of God's love as caring, giving, respecting, disciplining, and forgiving? Where do we each need to grow?

3. In what ways have we been pushed by our children to grow as parents and as persons of faith?

4. To what extent do we see and respond to our children as gifts from God?

MEDITATION

O God,
   I am your child.
   My spouse is your child.
   Your love for us is perfect.
      You care for us . . . give to us . . . respect us . . .
        discipline us . . . forgive us.

      Great is your love for us.

   Guide us as we faithfully show something of that
      love to our children.
      May we obediently teach them your ways.
      Thank you for the gift of children in our lives.
   Amen.

CHAPTER 12

NURTURING FAITH THROUGH SHARED EXPERIENCES

REFLECTION

Three Life Stories

The Holy Land trip had been planned for months. Finally, the time came. Their first trip to Gordon's Calvary (The Garden Tomb) was a disappointment. There were people everywhere. Tour groups, one after the other, were getting their pictures taken.

A specially arranged visit just before dawn the next morning was a stark contrast. The air was brisk, the paths empty, and the garden quiet. They walked in silence until they found a place to sit. Not a word was spoken. Forty minutes passed as they watched the sun climb into full view above the horizon. They clasped hands as they walked to the tomb and entered to stand where the body of Jesus had once lain. They were overwhelmed by emotion. Tears streamed down their cheeks. The power of the resurrection and its meaning for their lives was experienced in vital new ways in that setting at that time. They might never again visit the Holy Land together. But they had shared an awesome, life-affirming experience. They had hardly spoken a word. However, they knew that God was present in a new, more powerful way in their lives and in their relationship. The meaning was in being there together.

* * * * *

When their first son was born, Pat was whisked away to the delivery room and Bob was directed to the fathers' waiting room. The minutes stretched into an eternity for Bob. Finally, the word came that the baby boy was delivered and the mother was fine. Relief! Joy! Excitement! He was allowed to gaze at the wonder of his son through the nursery window. Eventually, he was permitted to be with Pat in her room.

Seven years later, when their second child was delivered, things were done differently. Bob and Pat had attended natural childbirth classes. Bob encouraged and enabled Pat's progress as she moved through labor. He was in the delivery room—present with Pat as she pushed and strained, present as their baby daughter took her first breath and gave her first cry, present to hold the new baby, present to draw Pat into his arms as tears streamed down their faces. There were few words spoken. Words were inadequate. Pat and Bob were together. The meaning was in the shared experience.

Later, both Pat and Bob talked about the joy and ecstasy of those precious moments. Not only did they treasure being together, but also pointed beyond themselves to God's presence and action. They searched for ways to describe what had transpired. Each said to the other, "I know what you mean!" Several years after the event, tears still came readily as Pat or Bob described their sense of togetherness and oneness in those moments.

* * * * *

We have vivid memories of being together at a marriage enrichment event led by David and Vera Mace, who at that time had been married forty-seven years. One morning during the retreat, they demonstrated for the group a faith ritual which was part of their daily life. They began by reading a short passage of Scripture. Then they sat in silence for a while. Each one jotted down some thoughts as these came into their thinking. Breaking the silence, they talked about some of the items on the list. David's health was on both lists. David reported that he knew Vera expended considerable energy in concern and worry about his physical condition. He smiled at her and commented, "Vera, you don't need to do that because I want you to. But I know you do it because of your love for me, and I thank you for that."

Vera acknowledged his statement, and reported that one of the more difficult parts of growing older was facing the reality that they had a limited number of days, months, or years left to share together. She smiled then and said seriously, "David, I consider every day we have together a gift of God. These are precious days. Every minute is important." He reached out to pat her hand in a gesture of agreement. They looked into each other's eyes for a long moment. Then they moved on to discuss another item.

Through our own tears, we (Myron and Jan) looked at each other. It was as if we were standing on sacred ground and sharing holy moments with this couple and with each other. David and Vera were nurturing each other in the faith required by old age. In the process of their sharing, they were nurturing us, who are middle-aged.

Sharing the Requirements of Living

As a couple walk together through the minutes, hours, days, weeks, months, and years, they build a history of life experiences. Many of these seem terribly routine—setting the alarm, switching it off, starting the coffee, doing the grocery shopping, removing the trash, putting the cap on the toothpaste, changing the sheets, cleaning the bath, preparing food—the list is endless. Every couple develops their own agenda of necessities. For most couples, the list gets divided up between them in some workable way. "You do some and I'll do some" is a common contract, frequently not verbalized, but operating with great force and regularity. These tasks are shared in the sense that we both invest our energy in these things that have to be done. But this "sharedness" has nothing to do with the actual performance of the responsibilities. In fact, when I carry out the trash, change the bed, clean the toilet, or clear the table, I feel very much alone. My spouse is involved elsewhere and I may begin to wonder if there is anything we share that really draws us close together. Getting these tasks done surely doesn't.

It takes a conscious effort to maintain a sense of togetherness in the context of life's nitty-gritty details. Life will become miserable very quickly if the essentials don't get done. They demand a certain amount of time and energy.

There are some things we can ponder to help us keep a shared perspective. I do many things, for example, because I love my spouse and I love our life together. I want us to grow and change and deepen our relationship. Persevering in doing the necessities helps free us to do that. My actions grow out of that love. I need to tell my spouse occasionally what a drag these tasks become, and that it's my love that keeps me hanging in there. It is equally important for me to recognize that hanging in can be demanding, draining, and terribly boring for my partner. I should express gratitude for my partner's willingness to do these things out of love for me and our shared life. Such mutual expressions of appreciation can remind us of our shared life in the midst of the mundane.

Also, it can prove helpful for couples to examine their list of necessities. Some of the requirements may not actually have to be there. Perhaps they have found their way onto that list through habit. If the list can be pruned, time will be freed for more rewarding life experiences.

It eased our load a bit for example when we decided that the beds could be changed every other week rather than weekly. We sometimes lighten our load considerably by reviewing all the tasks and asking ourselves a few questions: Are these *really* necessities? Who requires them? How often? Could they be done more quickly or easily? I am made more aware that we are sharing life when we take this kind of "inventory" time together. It's when things go on "as usual" month after month, year after year, that I begin to wonder.

Many couples might achieve some variety by occasionally reassigning who does what. For years, Jan had been responsible for setting the alarm, pulling the plug, and shutting it off in the morning as quickly as possible. One night, she thought about having that responsibility as long as our life together lasted. It was a small thing, but in that long-range perspective, it seemed overwhelmingly heavy. We talked about it and Myron moved the alarm to his side of the bed. That was several years ago. In doing that, he communicated to Jan, "I want to share life experiences with you. I can do that." Very likely, the alarm will eventually come back to Jan's side for a season. But the weight will be lightened because it has been shared.

Not all things can be reassigned as easily as an alarm clock. Some do not lend themselves to change at all. "You do this and I'll do that" on such tasks may, indeed, not apply. Yet many couples may discover they can be far more flexible than they are. They may have become stuck as if cement anchored their behavior.

Occasionally, we have found some meaningful togetherness when we have decided (often spontaneously) to share a required task. Myron does a great deal of our banking and shopping. Somehow, it seems extra special when Jan chooses to take the time to go along. During the summer months, Jan likes to hang the clothes on the line to dry and it feels good when Myron helps with this.

Sometimes, however, sharing required tasks has caused a problem. One spouse may volunteer to assume some new responsibility and begins to do it. The other spouse steps in and trys to correct the manner in which it is being done. "I'm really glad you're willing to do the job, but you need to do it my way or it won't be done right," says the spouse implicitly. Right means "my way." The other spouse soon becomes discouraged and may even back away entirely.

What started out as a positive thing failed miserably. Marriage partners are not identical people. We are failing to put our understanding into operation if we do not allow our spouse to be free as a person to get the job done. Tasks which require strict performance must be carefully and patiently taught. A spouse who is just beginning can't be expected to perform as perfectly as one who has done the job over months or years.

Because so much marital time is consumed by the "have-to-get-dones," it's crucial that couples acknowledge and cultivate a sense of togetherness in the midst of their routines. This challenge may prove difficult, but we can not overestimate its importance to our relational well-being.

Sharing the Never-to-be-Forgottens

The three experiences described in the opening of this chapter were the kind which become relational highlights bonding persons to a deeper togetherness for the duration of their life. Every couple develops a history of never-to-be-forgotten moments when their being together was something indescribable, when they could sense and feel their oneness. When asked to describe such events, most couples protest that it's impossible to talk about what happened. Somehow, words trivialize the deep significance. In trying to isolate certain aspects of the experience, couples stress the tangibility of the oneness they knew. They felt a compelling togetherness—"almost as if we were melted together or fused."

Yet, in the midst of this oneness, they will note how they were also very conscious of their individuality. There seems to be no contradiction between these two experiences. "At the time we were most together and conscious of being 'we,' there was also a sense of 'I as I' and 'you as you.' " It is common for couples to note that during these experiences, besides being aware of their togetherness, they also sensed a presence beyond themselves in the midst of it all—God. It's as if there were a heightened awareness at three different levels: I as I, I as together with you, I as linked to God in a special way.

These experiences of being together are important for building and nurturing a relationship. Through them, intimacy and closeness are validated. We come away with renewed energy to face the routine and mundane. Our faith in God and trust in each other are rekindled. Joy pervades our being together in life. Our love for each other is deepened.

Building a Relational History of Shared Experiences

Most of us would recognize that it's foolish to advise all couples to "plan for these events at specified and regular intervals." They don't happen that way. Sometimes they come alongside other life experiences, like the birth of a baby. Other times, they occur as isolated events. For the most part, they are spontaneous—treasured gifts given for a particular time and space.

While couples cannot formulate a plan which guarantees heightened togetherness, it's crucial that they take time to be available to each other. When couples neglect being together, the possibility of intense shared experiences is reduced. Obviously, more is involved than just being present in the same space. Mutual expressions of warmth, acceptance, care, love, commitment, and trust are also crucial. It's difficult, if not impossible, to feel bound together intensely if we are feeling distraught, unaccepted, rejected, alienated, or angry. If a couple discovers that much of their relationship is being lived out in the context of negative attitudes and feelings about themselves and their relationship, they will not experience vital or intense experiences together.

Yet, shared moments offer the opportunity for couples to be bound together in deeper and more significant ways. Persons dominated by negative attitudes may find it helpful to work at practicing thinking positively about each other and their relational strength while together. Sometimes, it helps to reach back in an effort to recapture feelings we had for each other and for our relationship around the time of our wedding. Being reminded of those feelings may help us to discover that they aren't dead now. They have somehow gotten pushed aside and buried by other things.

Intensely shared experiences are unique to each couple. Becoming captured by a symphony in the summer air, reaching the top of a mountain after a long hike, driving the last nail which finishes the family room paneling, eating dinner at a fine restaurant to mark a wedding anniversary, participating in the celebration of the Lord's Supper together—each couple creates a relational history of shared experiences. The history may not always be made up of earthshaking events. Coming together sexually may have unusually intense dimensions which make us aware in new ways of our togetherness. It's the being together, however it's done, that signals to us that we really do share life.

Shared Experiences and Faith

Shared experiences and faith interact in an interesting way. Sometimes in practicing our faith together, at home or in the faith community, intense moments are experienced or we are made more conscious of being together in the midst of the routine. An important factor to keep in mind is that part of our faith practice needs to be done together. We will grow in our faith and in our togetherness because we actually participate as persons of faith together. In situations where the faith of the two persons is very different, it may help to focus on the dimensions of faith which unite them, letting the differences slide into the background for a period of time. If such couples maintain the differences as primary, they may lose any opportunity to grow together in faith. Affirming those aspects of faith which unite may surprisingly awaken us to see that we are more together than our differences make us feel. If I'm different from you, perhaps it will help me understand you and myself better if I allow myself to engage in practicing faith your way for a period of time. Likewise, you might allow yourself to be alongside me in a similar way.

Intense shared moments often raise a consciousness of the presence of God in the participants. Our togetherness can grow during these experiences; so can our faith. It may be helpful to reflect on the meaning of the event for us as a couple, but also for us as people of faith. We may discover that a faith relationship which had been taken for granted or ignored has been rekindled in a new way.

Shared experiences are a gift. Part of the gift is from each person to the other—being available, being open, being with the other. The greater part is God's gift to us. God has given us all of life and its relationships. Consequently, thanksgiving appropriately follows such experiences.

It is a time of saying "Thank you, God,

> for life,
> for my spouse,
> for myself,
> for our life together.

In the midst of routine and mundane tasks, it may be more difficult to cultivate an awareness of God's presence. Centuries ago, Brother Lawrence discovered the importance of practicing the presence of God in all of life. God's presence can be found in preparing the meals, washing the dishes, cleaning the car, or whatever. Our strength comes as a gift from the living God. As we are aware of God's presence in the whole of life, our togetherness—in the heightened moments and the routine tasks—takes on new depth and significance.

EXERCISE

1. Make a "history" of your heightened togetherness moments, starting from before marriage to the present. Take some time to talk about their meaning to you. Use this opportunity to say thank you to each other and to God.

2. List the required tasks of your life together. Discuss the following questions: Who requires each task? Who does it? How flexible can we be in doing each task? How might we be more affirming of each other for investing energy in routine things? How consciously grateful are we for the strength God supplies to us daily?

3. Schedule some concrete time blocks for simply being together. Commit yourselves to being present to each other at given times. Choose activities you really want to do together.

MEDITATION

Oh God, when I think of the many required, routine things we do to keep our marriage going, I become weary. Sometimes I wonder if it's worth it all. I can really get bogged down.

BUT

If I think deeper, I begin to realize that it's our mutual love for each other that keeps us going. It's your love for us that sustains us and gives us strength. And I thank you for these gifts, Lord.

AND

I remember those special times when we have felt so much together that a mysterious sense of oneness hovered around us. I remember being aware of your presence in a special way. Oh God, I am grateful for these precious relational moments in our marriage. Thank you for life and the people who share life with me.

A prayer to say together:

She: I thank God for you, _____
                                          husband's name

He: And I thank God for you, _____
                                          wife's name

Together: We thank you, Lord, for each other, and for your presence in our life. Amen.

CHAPTER 13

NURTURING FAITH THROUGH MUTUAL SERVICE

REFLECTION

In the Old Testament, God told Israel they were a servant people, a light to the nations. They were to be his own people. Jesus told his disciples that they were salt, leaven, and light in a needy world. They were to go and preach the good news of the gospel. They were to give drink to the thirsty, food to the starving, freedom to the enslaved, clothes to the naked, love to the unlovable, and care to the widows and orphans. The Christian faith has always been, when properly understood and lived, a faith which reaches beyond itself to the needs of others.

Serving the Needs of Others

The themes in this book have focused primarily on the inner dynamics of the marriage relationship. This final theme will speak of turning outward as God's people to service beyond ourselves and our own needs. Caring for and giving attention to our marital relationship is worthy of our time and energy and is essential to faithful discipleship. But it's not sufficient for Christ's disciples. There must also be a turning outward toward others and their needs.

Healthy Marriages and Community Involvement

Perhaps it should not surprise us, given the servant emphasis in our faith, that social scientists are discovering that one mark of a healthy family is its involvement in and contribution to the community where it lives. Some families open their doors and absorb others into their family life. Others become active in school and their places of employment. Still others participate as family units in civic affairs of one kind or another. Some may combine all of these activities into a pattern which fits them. The important point is that somehow these families find time and energy to contribute to the well-being of others. The forms and ways of service vary radically. Healthy families find a way to do it.

Unhealthy Involvement

It should be emphasized that the outward service shouldn't be at the expense of the family's or marriage's well-being. Sometimes persons turn outward to avoid responsibility within the marital or family relationship. Occasionally, active persons may not realize the amount of energy they are spending beyond their marriage and that they are really neglecting their primary relationship. The following are examples of unhealthy outward turnings.

A husband/father was discontented with his home life. He was in constant conflict with his wife and teenage children, and began spending greater amounts of time at the school where he taught. In this way, he successfully avoided the troubles at home. He became a stranger to his own family. His wife voiced her feeling of betrayal: "He's given me up for his job. It's like I'm not married anymore." This man was turned outward, but it wasn't healthy.

Another couple was almost ready to launch the last of their four children from home. In raising four teenagers, they had become very involved alongside each one in various kinds of activities—regular schoolwork, music, sports, drama, and student government. For over a decade, they had given themselves completely to the schedules set by four growing youth. It had been fun and rewarding. They had made many friends. The time seemed well spent. However, they soon realized they had failed to keep up with changes in each other. They had accumulated a backlog of feelings about which they had never found time to talk. What had begun so innocently in an effort to be good parents had a negative result. In giving time to the children and their activities, they had not scheduled enough for each other. This couple was turned outward but it had become unhealthy.

Balancing Inward and Outward Commitments

While our faith calls us to contribute to the needs and well-being of others, we must balance this with investment in our marriage, its nurturing, its vitality. To turn outward without keeping an inward awareness is to drain the health of a marriage.

The inward and outward awarenesses feed into each other. A healthy marriage relationship builds personal and relational resources which flow out to others. In turn, giving and contributing to those beyond themselves generate new energies for the couple to give to each other. The balance, if kept, can lead to many years of fulfillment.

Discovering Our Gifts

Service challenges Christians to consider the gifts and abilities they have been given. Each one must ask, "How can I best serve? What are my gifts? What are my abilities?" Spouses should be able to see the gifts of their mate better than anyone else. Sometimes, persons need to be invited to develop their gifts. Marriage companions can be an effective channel for that invitation. They can be sensitive in challenging the other in ways which gently push but do not frighten.

You may remember from our discussion of self-esteem that many adults do not believe in their own value. They think others have much more to contribute to life than they do. They don't see nor own the gifts they have been given. Spouses can support their mate in the struggle to cultivate feelings of self-worth. As self-esteem is strengthened, so is the capacity to recognize, own, and use one's gifts.

Individual Service

Service can be performed individually. Each partner becomes involved in activities quite apart from the other. Yet, even when the service is performed by one spouse rather than the other, there's a need for mutuality. Giving of oneself can be draining. Frustrations can mount. When no overt appreciation is shown, feelings of despair and futility may emerge. So it is a source of comfort and security to know one's spouse is interested and supportive. I need my partner to listen, to encourage, to give suggestions (when I'm ready), to help, and sometimes to actually stand alongside me.

Unfortunately, some couples are unaware that separate involvement in service still demands considerable mutual support. Sometimes the mate may even become antagonistic, seeing that the other has separate service involvements. Feelings of jealousy may surface because the spouse thinks that time and energy invested in behalf of others should be directed inward. When this kind of pressure develops, both persons need to clarify, understand, and renegotiate their relationship, and the place service has in it.

One husband became involved in coaching Little League baseball when his son joined. Having been a fine athlete during his school years, his abilities were soon noted. He liked teaching the youngsters and helping them perfect their skills. Soon he was involved in other sporting programs. Many weeknights and Saturdays throughout most of the year were scheduled. He enjoyed it and felt good about what he was doing. However, his wife began to develop more and more negative feelings. She liked sports, too, but this frantic pace began to be too much. She was doing most of the household tasks and transporting the children to their various activities. When she found it necessary to drop out of some of her own involvements, she began to question the entire situation. She confronted her husband directly. He seemed shocked: "I thought you were with me in this." "I *was,*" she said, "but it's too much. Can't you see that?" This was the beginning of much talk which led to a more balanced situation for both spouses. Anger and resentment stem from feelings of being unfairly treated.

Service rendered by either spouse can nurture the faith of both. If couples affirm the abilities of each other and use them in behalf of others, their faith will be enriched.

Rosie was the coordinator of a summer activities program for middle school-aged children in her church. The program's purpose was to reach children in the neighborhood who were unreached by the church. No one knew what response would be achieved. Rosie put in a great deal of effort throughout the summer. Her husband, John, was unable to help because of his job. The program reached many children. The first Sunday in September two of the children from the summer program came for church school and worship. Both John and Rosie were delighted. They felt Rosie's investment of time and energy was worth it. The sight of the two children was their mutual reward for Rosie's exercise of faith.

Mutual Service

Service can be rendered by a couple together. There are many ways to become involved on behalf of others. Caring for foster children can be a long-term commitment. Other kinds of service are short-range. Each couple has to find their own way in accord with their own interests, gifts, and circumstances. The critical first step is to commit a portion of their time together to help others.

When our son, Tim, was small, Jan began teaching two mornings a week. We needed someone to care for him. We discovered an elderly couple who opened their home to five or six two- and three-year-old children, providing daily care at inexpensive rates. They called their endeavor Little Chaps School. Tim loved it. One day when picking Tim up, Jan asked the woman about the school. She smiled and said, "Well, our own grandchildren live across the country. We don't see them very often. We love kids. So, we decided to start the school. We can help young couples get started. We give the kids lots of love and attention. Besides, the kids keep us young." She was right. They were a very youthful couple in their seventies.

The Rewards of Service

Why is service so necessary? This is a good question. The most direct response is that it's necessary because our Lord commanded it. That is a sufficient reason in itself. If we want to be faithful, true disciples, we must be obedient in our faith walk. Our faith pilgrimage is one of service in behalf of humankind. We're called to be bearers of the Good News, in both word and action. There is no guarantee that our obedient life will lead to special rewards or favors from God. To the contrary, a life of service may call for sacrifice and suffering on our part. God's promise is to be with us and to keep us in a loving relationship with himself.

However, we have received significant rewards from many of our service involvements. Through our giving and investment of self, a return has come. It's unexpected and usually not at all what we had anticipated, but rewarding nonetheless.

Several years ago, our family attended an annual ecumenical conference in clown, mime, puppet, and dance ministry. At a workshop, one couple in their early sixties told of how they had been serving in clown ministry for over five years. When she had begun to train as a clown, make her costume, design her face, and develop her character, he had thought the entire thing silly and fanciful. "If she wanted to do it, okay," he said, "but I wanted to be left out of it. She went to local hospitals and nursing homes for over a year. I thought she was on a kick. But then she began to tell me of some of the things that happened. One day I went with her." He stopped and grinned at her, then added, "I've been going ever since. She rarely does a clowning thing without me." They joined in telling about the joy they had been able to bring into the lives of despairing, hopeless people. He had become a clown himself, although he often went without costume. "I like to talk to the people. She goes ahead of me and gets them to laugh a little. I come along and chat. Sometimes I just listen. We make a good team." Their ministry now covers a region of several hundred miles. Someone in the workshop asked, "What's in it for you? Why do you do it?" Her response was quick, "Well, we do it because it's our ministry, but it's strange. As we bring happiness to them, a certain joy comes home to us." Their glowing joyful faces confirmed the truth in her comment.

There is joy in the act of giving. This, surely, is one reward of service.

For us, the learning we have gained has been a primary reward of service. When Myron was a campus chaplain in the 1960s, racial issues rocked the country. The day before freshman orientation was to begin on campus, Jan answered a knock at our front door. A black woman stood there with a youth shyly peering around the corner. She explained their situation. Earlier in the summer, they had rented a room and placed a deposit to hold it for fall because they couldn't afford dorm costs. When they returned later, the landlord politely explained that her neighbors had threatened her for renting to a black. Apologetically, she gave back the deposit money. The mother went on to say how important a college education was for her son. Her oldest daughter was a college graduate and had secured a good job. "Without a college education, they can't go nowhere!" she emphasized. She asked a quick question: "Can he stay with you until we can work something out?" We agreed. It was the beginning of a two-year stay for Garfield in our home.

During that time, we learned lessons which continue to shape our lives today. We soon realized that when he went out to dinner with us, we were seated in the back, less obvious section. When we went by ourselves, it didn't seem to matter. White students could get haircuts at the local barber shops. Blacks could not. The barbers didn't know how to cut "their woolly hair," and didn't want to learn. These were two of the early lessons. We learned, too, that the black mother had been right. Some of his friends who weren't getting an education seemed to be going nowhere. But he *has* gone somewhere. From college, he entered law school and today he is a lawyer, a husband, and a father of three small children. *He is somewhere.*

As we have reached out in service, we have met some beautiful people who in one way or another have impacted our lives. We began by moving out to serve and meet their needs. We discovered persons who in turn served us. We have been changed by them. Sometimes we meet them simply in a passing encounter. At other times, they become lifelong friends.

We have been rewarded many times for our service. Sometimes the rewards outweigh the investment or cost to self that we have made. We've grown in the serving. Of course, our intense involvement in giving has sometimes caused us to neglect each other. Then we have had to back away and take another look at ourselves, our relationship, and our service commitment. It hasn't always been easy to decide how much is enough or how much is too much.

Our Lord has called us to service. How are you serving—as an individual, as a couple? How is service enriching your faith?

Opportunities for Service

As couples commited to a faith relationship with the living Christ, one of our tasks is to find opportunities for service. Once we have assessed our gifts, we need to find those opportunities in which we can put our faith to work. Some of the searching will be for ourselves, some for our spouses, and some for mutual involvement. As we give ourselves to the needs and well-being of others, we will discover the truth of a basic faith principle taught by our Lord: "Anyone who wants to save his life will lose it; but anyone who loses his life for my sake will find it" (Mt 16:25).

EXERCISE

Instructions: Complete Item 1 separately. Take some time to discuss the gifts you see in each other. Then proceed with Items 2 through 4 as a couple.

Husband
1. These are gifts and talents I think you have for serving others:

Wife
1 . These are gifts and talents I think you have for serving others:

2. These are ways we are using our gifts and talents for serving others:
   Wife:

   Husband:

   Couple:

3. These are ideas for service involvement we would like to try in the future:
   Wife:

   Husband:

   Couple:

4. Specific commitments we would like to make are:

MEDITATION

We love because he first loved us. If anyone says, 'I love God,' and hates his brother, he is a liar; for he who does not love his brother whom he has seen, cannot love God whom he has not seen. And this commandment we have from him, that he who loves God should love his brother also.

I John 5:19-21

O God, help us to use our gifts and our talents to love and serve others in your name.

O God, help us. We give our lives to you. Amen.

Afterword

In this book, we've offered you several themes around which to think about your faith and marriage. We could have developed many others, but in our minds these thirteen themes with the exercises and meditations are powerful nutrients for enriching marriage and nurturing faith.

As you and your spouse have read, talked, listened, and meditated, it has been our prayerful hope that something positive has occurred in your relationship with each other, and in your faith relationship with God. It has also been our wish that as you come to the end of this faith pilgrimage together, you'll want to return to some of the topics and experience them again, but in new and deeper ways.

With the above having been said, our final prayer meditation for you and us is the following:

> O Lord of our marriage,
>   May your creative Spirit
> Go before us to guide us,
> Be above us to enlighten us,
> Be behind us to protect us,
> Be beneath us to support us,
> Be beside us to befriend us,
> Be between us to bond us together, and
> Be within each of us to give us peace.
> Amen!